Come Monday

My Journey on
The Pink Ribbon Road

A Memoir By
Carolyn Mustian

MondaysJourney.com

Come Monday
My Journey on The Pink Ribbon Road

©2012 by Carolyn Mustian
Published 2012 by Carolyn Mustian Books, LLC

ISBN: 978-0-9856021-0-9

Contact the publisher at: CarolynMustian@msn.com

Scripture taken from the HOLY BIBLE, NEW INTERNATIONAL VERSION®. Copyright© 1973, 1978, 1984 by International Bible Society. Used by permission of Zondervan Publishing House. All rights reserved.

The "NIV" and "New International Version" trademarks are registered in the United States Patent and Trademark Office by International Bible Society. Use of either trademark requires the permission of International Bible Society.

Editing, layout cover design, publishing consulting and author coaching provided by Alane Pearce, Author Coach at Alane Pearce Professional Writing Services AlanePearce.com.
Turning Writers into Published and Promoted Authors
alane@AlanePearce.com

Mustian, Carolyn: Come Monday: A Journey on The Pink Ribbon Road
1. Nonfiction/Memoir 2. Women's Issues/Breast Cancer
3. Christian/Inspirational

This book is dedicated to my sweet husband, Ward,
who is my encourager in all things,
and to my dear sisters on the Pink Ribbon Road.
One day I hope no one needs to travel it!

July 12, 2012

Warm Wishes,

Carla Mustin
Psalm 16

Table of Contents

Preface

I did not begin 2010 with the expectation of going on a life journey of such great proportions. But 2010 became a life changing year when I was diagnosed with breast cancer just one week into the New Year. Nevertheless, it became a year of great lessons and blessings as I navigated the strange waters of a disease which has become all too common in today's world. Fortunately, I did not have to walk this journey alone. I was accompanied by precious women who had walked ahead of me on the pink ribbon road. In addition, I was blessed with an amazing medical team cobbled together from a variety of practices and settings. Furthermore, I was blessed with the care, encouragement and prayers of family, friends and strangers who made time to hold me in their hearts. I invite you to take a look into my world as I recorded my experiences along this way.

However, I do have some warnings for you. Most of the materials in this book are journal entries I wrote during the treatment process. I tried to stay true to what I was experiencing at the moment; therefore, the entries are in no way intended to be used as medical advice, nor are my moments of frustration an indictment of the wonderful people who provided care for me. Sometimes I was frustrated by a situation I felt could have been handled better, but sometimes I was the one who should actually have been handling things better. I have simply recorded my experiences and emotions as honestly as I could as they were originally reflected in my thoughts and feelings at the moment. In a few cases, I have added a section of reflection or updates to clarify something that eventually looked to me like a misconception on my part, or lack of understanding of how medical care is delivered today. After all, I graduated from nursing school in 1980 and left the health care profession as an employee about 10 years later. A lot has changed in the ensuing years and I experienced the impact of those changes.

I believe I was blessed with some of the best doctors and nurses and health care providers in the world. I also occasionally ran into some individuals I felt provided less than stellar care. It is important to recognize that selecting a medical team is a complicated process. Besides getting the most medically competent provider, one needs to have good rapport with one's caregivers. That means one needs a good fit between the personalities of the caregiver and the patient, as well as a good fit with the physical location where care is delivered. My city has several excellent cancer treatment centers and many very competent and talented physicians, nurses and other professionals who practice in all of these locations. The ones who cared for me are, in my opinion, some of the best there are, but that doesn't mean that those I didn't choose are less competent. It just means my providers were great fits for me. For these reasons, I have chosen not to use the names of those doctors providing care for me. The major point of this book is not to endorse nor condemn health care providers or places; instead, my purpose in publishing this book is to offer hope and encouragement to other women who may have to walk this route.

This book is also not intended to be a medical guide for making difficult decisions about treatment of a complicated disease. It is my understanding that breast cancer takes many forms. It also impacts one's perception of self and one's partner's perception of the one who gets the diagnosis. The treatment I chose was right for me but not necessarily right for others. There are many hard decisions that must be made relatively quickly when this disease presents. I have simply recorded my thought process as I made choices and looked for confirmation that I had made the right ones for me. But that does not mean that my decisions and choices are the best ones for the next woman who will have to make hard decisions about her treatment. Please read this book as my emotional and spiritual journey shared with the hope it will encourage and bless others who may be struggling with the hard facts of breast cancer or some other difficult life challenge. My journey became a year of blessings as well as challenges with humor sprinkled along the way as a delightful bonus.

Many times as I wrote, I also prayed. I have recorded my conversations with God in italics. These are not the only prayers I prayed during those long months, not by a long shot! But they are the prayers I prayed as I wrote in my journal. God faithfully answered and patiently taught me along the pink ribbon way. I am exceedingly grateful for his tender mercies toward me. I am also grateful for the sweet friends who walked along side me on this journey. In most cases I have used only their first names and in some cases I disguised their identity to protect their own story. In reality, I would be happy to post their names on big billboards because they have been great sources of blessing to me. But ultimately, I want my friends to feel safe interacting with me without the worry that they might end up in my next book! So, dear unnamed friends, thank you for your love and support!

Finally, there are some people I do want to thank publicly for their help and support in the publishing process. Thank you from the bottom of my heart to my sweet husband, Ward, and our sons, Andrew and David, for encouraging me all along this journey. Thank you for letting me run the risk of embarrassing you to tell my story, our family story, of a challenging year. Thank you, Sara Allen, for pouring over my manuscript and offering many helpful suggestions before it reached the hands of my coaching editor. Your willingness to dedicate hours of work on my manuscript while writing your own book is amazing to me. Thank you, Alane Pearce, author coach extraordinaire, for guiding me through the world of self-publishing and book promotion. You helped me make this dream come true!

Chapter One: JANUARY
Mammograms and Other Tests

January 5, Tuesday

This Does Not Look Good

Come Monday, I hope this will all be happily over and I'll be spreading the word that our God has healed me. Come Monday, I hope I will be a woman with a new lease on life, plans to make, dreams to fulfill, an old age to look forward to. I hope it will be glad Monday.

But this is Tuesday; the Tuesday after Sad Monday. The radiologist called it a mass, and I was not surprised. I saw it as the ultrasound technician marked it on her machine–the machine they send you to when the second set of digital mammogram images confirm the alarms the first ones raised. Not that I was taken totally by shock. After all, pain in my left breast sent me to visit my gynecologist's nurse practitioner a few days before Christmas. Although she felt no mass, this diagnostic mammogram was a precaution. A melanoma was removed from my arm last summer. And two aunts had recently died from cancer, one of them from breast cancer. I felt that I had moved from the category of a woman with no risk factors to one with glaring risks–a woman marked by genetics and probably too much sun bathing before we knew about sunscreens and cancer.

So I am not surprised, or even very hopeful of a good outcome. I've already been to the internet and realize that breast cancer which presents with pain is not usually the good kind to have. I know that there are few treatment options for metastatic melanoma, if that's what is growing there way too fast. The radiologist agreed with me when I used the word *aggressive*.

"It's not that it's so big," she said. "It's only 0.6 centimeters. It's that it appeared this large this fast. I went back to your mammogram from last year. There was nothing there–not even a shadow, just totally clear. It could be just a cyst, and we'll hope that's all it is," she suggested.

But I sensed that she really didn't think that was the case, and neither did I. Come Monday, I hope she and I are both happily wrong. But Monday seems a long way off. Today I will count my blessings and take comfort in the numbers of people who hold me in their prayers. I wrap myself in the prayers of the saints like a talisman or warm blanket to stave off the cold fear that nips at the edges of my peace. Usually a private person, I have guarded carefully my minor scrapes with illness, but this time I keep adding myself to prayer chains of friends, Bible study partners and any who would be willing to pray for me.

Tracy came to sit with me yesterday afternoon and offer the comfortable presence of a niece who loves me. Then she called today just to see how I am doing. She has been ill herself with so many maladies that I am thankful she has the energy to call. She will take me for my biopsy tomorrow and that is fitting. She's my daughter of my heart, the one my sister left me when she left this planet too soon herself. Sometimes women need other women with them, and tomorrow Tracy will be my companion, my sister in the Lord who will walk with me on this piece of my journey.

Last night, Tracy called and passed the telephone to her brother Michael Wayne. He said he had wanted to call but didn't know what to say. Then he thought about texting, but words eluded him in that medium as well. He told me for what it is worth that he said a prayer for me last night. For what it's worth! It's more precious than gold. *God, the prayers I've offered up to you for this nephew who struggles against himself, the pull of the world, and you. If this is what it takes to call him to prayer, thank you.*

Janet's phone call yesterday morning was both a blessing and a call to action. "Start writing," God seemed to speak to my heart, "because I'm going to surprise you with what I'm about to do." Her call was another confirmation that God has everything under control. And strangely, it was also perhaps God's whisper that this is not going to be an easy year. Come Monday, I will probably cry some more. I was supposed to teach Janet's Powhatan Community Bible Study® (CBS) class next Wednesday, but she called to say she is ready to resume her teaching role–the one I've filled for her since September while she helped her teenage son do battle with his own cancer demon. Janet had no idea that I was wondering what to do about next Wednesday. Janet, like nearly everyone I know, didn't even know I'd had a mammogram, much less a biopsy. I had been wondering what to do about next Wednesday's class. I didn't know if I would be able to concentrate enough to prepare a lecture, especially if the news is grim, or still uncertain. So God put it on her heart to call me and take back her rightful place a week early–thus blessing me, while also perhaps hinting at the inevitable as well. I also sensed that I'd better start writing down events of what was likely to be an eventful year.

I couldn't bring myself to call Ward after the mammogram because he had a boatload of his own patients to get through on his first day back to work after the holidays. "He deserves to get through this first long day without complications," I thought, even if the complication was me. I called Tracy, and she said she would be over in the afternoon, after her own doctor's appointment.

When I walked in the door at home, my son Andrew was rushing to get the old spa ready for removal before the electrician arrived to prepare for the new one arriving Wednesday. Then he and his brother David argued about whether Dave would help him outside in the bitter cold Virginia January. Next, Andrew's girlfriend showed up and I held my feelings in as long as I could, trying to move about normally in a world turned sharply on edge.

Finally, the dyke of pent up fearfulness–no, more accurately, sadness, and dread, like a hammer about to fall–began to leak around the edges. Andrew walked into the kitchen, saw me dressed up and said, "Where have you been today mom?"

"For a mammogram," I replied. He must have read some fear in my face.

"Is everything OK?" he asked.

"No," I answered with tears in my voice and eyes, but not yet on my cheeks.

"Come upstairs and talk to me," he replied.

And this time, I dutifully followed him up the steps, like a child follows her parent, roles reversed; but eager, actually, to tell someone face to face. As we stepped into my room, I began to cry, and he came and pulled me tightly to his chest. He held me and let me cry. How striking that it is my son who wipes my tears, hugs me tight, and longs to make everything right, as I did for him so many times when he was young.

But we're both adults now, and this threat is serious, not easily banished with a kiss on the boo-boo or a cookie or some other handy distraction. Still, for whatever time I have left, I will cherish that tender moment with my strong son's arms around me. We called David upstairs, and I told him my dreadful news. Both boys offered words of encouragement, and then David said, "Can I tell my praying buddies?"

"Of course you can," I answered.

And thus began the wrapping of myself in prayers. There's comfort knowing that I am wrapped in the blankets of prayer warriors whom I have never met. I think of the strangers I have prayed for because someone knew someone who knew me. And now I am some praying one's stranger and I'm thankful that someone knows someone who knows me. I am thankful that someone prays for David's mom, or Ward's wife, or her Community Bible Study® (CBS) sister, or a friend of a friend of a friend.

There was another prayer warrior who called me yesterday. As I stood in the Ukrops grocery line, where I had popped in after the mammogram to grab a few items, Alice Kish rang my cell phone to be sure I was still available to sub for the CBS home school teens on Thursday. Of the Christians I know, Alice was certainly one welcome voice. She has her own compelling story of God's grace and miracles extended to her son years ago during a farming accident. By all accounts, the accident should have been fatal. But he survived, and not only survived but thrives today–a nearly grown teen with no handicaps from the tractor, which ran over the little child's chest. I was glad to hear the voice of one who had faced death with the grace and power of God.

I cupped my hand around the phone and my mouth to speak quietly my dreadful news so strangers could not hear. "Don't cry," I silently prompted myself. Alice prayed for me as I clutched the phone and spoke powerful words of encouragement–scripture and blessing poured on a woman in shock. *Thank you, God that she called and prayed with me as I waited in that long line. You always have your people in place for the needs of the moment.*

Remembering...

Looking back over this now, I realized I didn't even have a record in my original journal of telling Ward about my mammogram. I think at least in part it was because I was so stunned and telling Ward was the hardest thing I had ever said to the man I love so dearly. I knew it would cut deep into his heart and I felt guilty, somehow, to be the cause of so much trouble. And perhaps, afraid that saying the words would make it more real and more dreadful–I was about to change both of our lives forever. So many unanswered questions, like a foggy monster, loomed over me. This is how I remember it now:

I couldn't call Ward while he was working. I know the pace he keeps as a dentist in solo practice and I just couldn't drop this bomb on him in the middle of a busy load of patients. This news would wait until he got home. Ward walked into the kitchen that evening as I hustled to get dinner ready. With the boys home from college, there is always extra activity buzzing in our household, no time to sit and lick my wounds, and I'm not even wired that way anyway. But, I'd held in this scary stuff for as long as I could, and I hated that the boys and I knew something that would have such a major impact on Ward, and he had no clue.

I turned from the oven to face Ward, who stood across the kitchen, still holding his briefcase and the day's mail. He sat them on the counter; I folded my arms across my chest, as though trying desperately to hold myself together. "Ward, they found a mass on the mammogram," I said. He folded his arms across his chest, mirroring my posture. We stood across from each other, maybe five or six feet apart, like two bookends– statutes for a moment frozen in time, just before plunging into uncharted waters. I think each of us willed ourselves to not fall apart for the other one. I don't remember much about what we actually said.

Like the two medical professionals that we are, I believe he asked some questions and I answered them, clinically, wooden. At some point, he hugged me, but my enduring memory of those first moments of telling was the image of each of us holding ourselves separately, tightly together as though if we moved, we would start spinning like an out of control top and just swirl off the planet in so many pieces. Somehow, I finished cooking, we sat down to dinner, and my men ate, but I don't think I actually tasted anything on my plate.

Casseroles and Appetite

This past week, I've been cooking casseroles, an answer to Dave's request for casseroles while he is home from college on winter break. "I'm sick of just plain food," he had said when he got home from Virginia Tech and so I've pulled out all my old standbys, which I rarely cook because they don't fit with the weight loss plan I have once again committed to for a season. But this week, since yesterday, overeating hasn't been a problem. I feel a little nauseous, and even when my stomach rumbles for food, nothing is appealing.

When my crying with the boys was over yesterday, I laughed and said, "Well, I guess I'm going to get slim now!" thinking about chemo and radiation and how much weight people lose when they are dying from cancer.

"Mom! Don't think like that! You don't even know the outcome of the tests yet–you don't know if this is really bad!" Andrew chastised me.

"That's true," I said. "I don't know, but deep in my soul, I don't have a good feeling about this. But maybe Monday will hold a wonderful surprise for me."

January 9, Thursday

Word of Knowledge

Today was a day of blessing in so many ways. I got to my Far West End Community Bible Study® (CBS) class near the end of leadership's pre-class prayer time. Although folks had already received my email prayer requests, I was immediately surrounded by women who wanted to comfort me and pray. They wrapped me in a cocoon of love and prayer and warm wishes. They listened to the tears of a mother's heart who fears leaving my boys so soon.

I have not feared my eternal destination; I know I will be held in the warm arms of my Savior. I haven't even feared the traumas of cancer; it is the potential good-byes that weigh so heavily on my heart; leaving loved ones with whom I want desperately to stay. It is the feeling of being a short-timer on planet earth that breaks my heart. And in my grief, I had lost my appetite. I have not been able to eat more than a few bites of food in the days since the mammography.

I went through my morning duties as a substitute core leader and really had fun filling in for the home school teen class. There were only three of them, but I loved ministering to them as an anonymous older woman, rather than the grieving mom I have become: they had no clue. Then came the lecture and I stayed in the sound booth, running the PowerPoint® for our teaching director as I normally do.

When the lecture ended, dear Pat came to me, dressed in her red mink coat, which always makes me smile and pet her back. But Pat is much more to me than a woman in a red mink coat. She has been my mentor and friend since we met my first year in CBS, back when Dave and Andrew were just 2 months and 15 months old, respectively. Last Thursday, Pat climbed into the sound booth, hugged me and said, "Carolyn, I think it's going to be all right. I just have this sense that you are going to be fine–it's going to turn out OK." Lots of ladies had said similar things that morning, but their words were prefaced with, "I hope, I pray …." Pat spoke with authority, like she had received a word from God. She had conviction in her voice, and for the first time that week, I dared to hope, really hope, that God would surprise me with good news. I felt calm. I ate lunch with leadership, like we do each Thursday afternoon. For the first time in days, food tasted delicious.

Pastor Phil called this evening with words of encouragement. I had spoken with his wife, Jody, about my new life challenge as we sat together at Wednesday night dinner at Gayton Baptist. She is a precious friend and she talked with me, and cried, and promised to pray–and I know she will. Then she asked if she could share with Phil, and of course I said yes. I'm still collecting my patchwork of prayers and they warm me deep in my spirit.

I am comforted that others are praying, because I am still struggling to know how to pray. Certainly I ask God for healing and health and life–more time with my men. And I know God is able to do all things, including heal me. I just don't know what he has planned for me. The Psalms say "*All my days were written for me in God's book before I was ever born.*" I think I'm paraphrasing somewhat, but that's the gist. I just don't know how many days he wrote, and so I don't know if his answers are "yes" or "no" when I ask for more time with my family here.

Shadrack, Meshach and Abednego were threatened with death in the fiery furnace of King Nebuchadnezzar if they did not bow down to his idol. And their response has been with me all week: "Our God is able to deliver us from the fiery furnace, O king, but even if he does not, we will not bow our knees to the idol."[1] I know my God is able to deliver me from this threat, I just don't know what he will choose to do. Nevertheless, I trust him.

When Phil talked with me, I shared this verse and my feelings about it with him. He told me he had been running, and praying for me, and listening to a teaching about suffering. The verse he listened to as he prayed for me was this very verse from Daniel! I was blown away! *You are good, God, you're really good at this stuff!*

January 8, Friday

D-Day

Today is D-Day–Diagnosis Day, the day I get results from the biopsy, three days earlier than the originally projected date of Monday. I have wanted this day to come, I need answers. But now it is here and for the first time I am filled with dread– dreading the answers I need, fearing the message the radiologist will deliver. Such a spirit of doom hangs over me because I expect the worst. And the sadness continues to wrap my heart in a dark and heavy blanket. If the news is bad, I'll cry, I'll grieve for those I love. I wanted more time–who doesn't? I wanted to celebrate my 50th wedding anniversary with Ward, but I'll hope to have the 25th this summer.

I am in a state of prayerfulness, but with no words. *Oh my God, thank you for the Holy Spirit who knows how to intercede for me.* My heart is breaking for my three precious men: Ward, love of my life; Andrew, my precious first born, so like me in determination, and intellect, except so much smarter; and David, my sweet second born, the one the doctor called my bonus baby when I got pregnant without needing fertility drugs, carefree David who makes me laugh.

---

1   Daniel 3:18

I worry for my father–83, I think–that he may lose me, too, and be left here alone because Catherine, Mother and I have all preceded him in death. How do I tell him the news? And Tracy and Michael Wayne, Catherine's children, the ones I have called the children of my heart since she died. Tracy said, "I can't lose another mother!" And I want to say, "God, did you hear her? Is this necessary?" But he's bigger than the both of us, and he sees and knows all. I must remind myself of this over and over if I'm starting down the road I think lies before me. Perhaps my most important role is to show her how to say goodbye. She didn't have that luxury when the auto accident snatched her mother away suddenly and far too young.

In fact, I said to Tracy, "Well, if this is it, at least I get to say goodbye."

And she said, "But Carolyn, you will have to suffer so. I don't want to see you suffer."

Frankly, I'm not anxious to suffer. I've often joked that on a scale of one to ten, all my pain is a ten. I'm God's great big wimp. I look anxiously for the rapture to rescue me and all my loved ones with me when life is hard. But suffering isn't necessarily the worst thing in the world. It can be a time of growth and maturity. *Oh God, make this journey before me a time to grow in your grace!*

It's Just Breast Cancer!

As D-day progressed, feelings of doom and sadness descended more heavily than before as I waited for the 2:30 appointment with the radiologist at the women's imaging center. Not knowing is a terrible limbo place to be. A feeling of nausea was my constant companion as I waited. This dread and anxiety is a more effective weight loss plan than any other I have found, but not so healthy, that's for sure.

Ward came home from work and we sat in the addition while I worked a jigsaw puzzle. The hands on the clock seemed to crawl backward as we waited to leave. I was actually anxious to get answers, even if they were the worst ones. It made a difference what I do next. We drove to the hospital, parked in the spaces reserved for the Women's Imaging Center and the Infusion Center and my thoughts drifted back to my years at the VA Medical Center where I had once helped the Chief of Oncology design and create a new Infusion Suite. Fast forward thirty years and I may be occupying just such a space myself.

Finally, the radiologist came into the room looking about the age of my sons, although I know he's actually thirty or thirty-one: The radiologist who conducted my biopsy had already prepared me for this young doctor to give me the test findings. Trying to be as gentle and kind as he could, to ease us into the results he was about to deliver, he said, "Well, you do have breast cancer, the garden variety kind that about 90% of women who get breast cancer have."

My response and that of my husband was one of near celebration. "Just breast cancer!" I exclaimed, "We can handle that!" or something like that. And we smiled at each other and breathed great sighs of relief. It was the doctor's turn to look shocked. Then I said, "You are positive it's not melanoma?" He had already explained to us that his delay in giving us the results was that the pathology department was still finishing up some tests. They had given him a preliminary verbal phone report. When I filled him in on the details of my recent cancer history, he telephoned back to pathology to confirm that it was not melanoma. I felt like I had won the lottery.

"I suppose you don't often have women happy to have breast cancer," I said, "but this is a much better diagnosis than melanoma. I feel like I have a fighting chance." He agreed with me and said this had happened to him once before with a woman battling lymphoma. Funny how one's perspective can alter one's response to what might normally be devastating news. As we entered the Woman's Imaging Suite, I noticed a woman just outside the door, with a look of brokenness on her face. I smiled, spoke and saw her chin tremble. I wanted to hug her and tell her it would be all right, supposing she had just gotten the news that she had breast cancer. Perhaps she wasn't a nurse like me, and so it may have taken her completely by surprise. But as I passed her I thought, "If I get the same news you probably just got, I'll be relieved."

I know I'm in giddy gladness right now. I am realistic enough to know the road is still going to be hard, but I've just been delivered from almost certain death to another chance at life. God gave me more time. I don't know how much, but likely more than I would have had with melanoma. With melanoma I would have been rushing to complete projects to leave my boys: photo albums, DVDs of old home movies, journals to edit. (I must edit–they don't need to know everything! But I do want to leave the life lessons God taught me.) I want to sew those slacks for Dad before I go to surgery–it could be a while before I can lift that heavy new machine I bought last summer. I'll still get on those projects quickly, no one is guaranteed tomorrow, but I'll be able to do them with less tears and sadness. I won't be saying goodbye with each task, but instead making plans to add to the project in the future.

I don't know what the surgeon will recommend, but my inclination at this moment is to have a double mastectomy. I don't think I want to have to worry about a recurring aggressive cancer. Ward immediately supported my decision and I know I'm blessed to have him for my husband. Some men bail on wives with this diagnosis. Instead we joked that it is true, spouses do look more and more alike as they grow older. We'll probably both be bald and flat chested before this journey is over. In fact, when I said that, Ward protested with mock indignity: "Wait a minute–I'm not flat-chested! I work out all the time." And that's true, he has great pecks. And I may finally get my Dolly Parton's in reconstruction!

How odd that I'm probably going to lose my breasts. I just made peace with them a couple of years ago. From the time I was a teen, I was disappointed to be small breasted. So at 28 or 29, I got implants. That was back in the early days of breast augmentation and women didn't have much say in what size they got–it was the surgeon's decision–and he made me way too small for my taste. For all that pain and money, I barely got one cup size bigger. Fast forward to two summers ago when one of the implants deflated, causing me to have to have both removed. I had the option to get new implants but decided to be happy with the breasts God gave me. The surprise was that my smaller breasts did make me look slimmer–not a bad trade-off for a woman who has also always struggled with weight issues. Now I may actually come out on the other side of this adventure slim and busty! *God, you are so funny! You have such a sense of humor! Remind me to keep laughing on the hard days of this journey. And please keep whispering your little bits of humor in* my ear!

Puzzles

When I was growing up, we used to work jigsaw puzzles in my family. Mother would put up a card table in the living room and we followed a set process. Dump out all the pieces and turn them face up. Separate out the border's straight edges and work that first. Only then would we think about the rest of those puzzle pieces. Usually each of us would pick a color or object in the puzzle and find the parts that seemed to relate. Years later, when Mother struggled with the handicaps of stroke and osteoporosis, I began to bring her small jigsaw puzzles to occupy her time. She said they saved her life.

I have continued to enjoy jigsaw puzzles but only permit myself the luxury of working them when it snows and life slows to a crawl, or when I'm at the beach condo. I allow myself the leisure to work jigsaw puzzles there, especially now that I avoid big doses of sun exposure.

So this week, as I waited for tests and results, I worked a jigsaw puzzle. It was more challenging than those we worked when I was a child-a 1000 piece "world's smallest". It kept my hands and mind busy, but it also became a framework for prayer and planning and grieving. I remember my mother saying that she preached her best sermons over the ironing board and I suppose the jigsaw puzzle was my ironing board this week. I sorted thoughts while I searched for that elusive puzzle piece. If my journey takes me down the road of surgery, chemo, radiation or all of the above, I'll probably work a lot of jigsaw puzzles in the months to come. One can work a lot of prayer into a jigsaw puzzle. Thank goodness the store had several of these! Besides, I'm getting the impression that walking down this cancer road is sort of like working a jigsaw puzzle, one section at a time.

January 11, Monday

Glad Monday

Thank you, God, for Glad Monday. I wasn't sure I would have one-in fact, I was pretty sure this would be Sad Monday. Thank you that you have turned my mourning into joy!

I am amazed at the outpouring of love which rushes in on all sides of me. Sunday morning was especially poignant. When the Sunday service was over, a number of people practically rushed to my side. Some of them are breast cancer survivors themselves. Each one was eager to hug me or to squeeze my hand, to offer words of encouragement, promises of prayer, and practical help. I knew there would be offers of meals, drives to the doctor, but some of these women were way ahead of me in awareness of my needs.

"Do you have a regular house cleaner, or do you do your own

cleaning?" one woman asked.

"I do my own," I replied, and I should have added, "And not nearly often enough!"

"I'm really good at cleaning toilets!" she offered, and I could hear in her voice that she meant it.

I was especially blessed by the women who have walked this very road, some of them rather reserved by nature. Yet they offered all of themselves to me, ready to answer any questions, and they emphasized "any". They were gracious to share their knowledge of doctors and treatments and other events on this pathway. I was struck by each woman's willingness, even eagerness, to make herself accessible to me in whatever way I needed her.

I thought back to the previous week and remembered my phone conversation with a woman whom I had probably seen only a couple of times in the past twenty-five years. We had been in a Bible study together many years before, but when a mutual friend heard my news, she put Brenda and me in touch right away. In one quick phone call, Brenda answered so many questions including some very personal ones about reconstruction options. She works in women's health and so she is in a place to have quick and current answers. But her most valuable words came from her heart and her own personal journey. And as we hung up, she offered these words, or something like them: "You are starting on an amazing journey, and it will be one of many blessings." Funny, one wouldn't normally anticipate a trip down breast cancer lane as an amazing journey of blessings; in fact, I've already been showered with blessings and I'm only a week along the voyage.

As Jeremiah records God's words: "…For I know the plans I have for you," says the Lord. "Plans to bless you and not harm you, plans to give you hope and a future."[2] I have always had hope and a future with God through Jesus Christ, and I will

---

2   *Jeremiah 28:11*

continue to have both of those, whether here on earth or in heaven, but Pat's words last Thursday, and the prayers of the saints surrounding me at the CBS luncheon permitted me to dare to hope that my near future will be on earth, watching my boys move through young adulthood. I recently heard someone say "God is good, all the time." *Yes, you are Lord, yes you are.*

And today, I celebrate Glad Monday. I'm not naive. I know that breast cancer is a battle against a formidable enemy. I know my God holds my life in his hands; he wrote my days in his book. But today I dare to hope he has left a lot of days for me still to live with my earthly family. *Thy will be done, Heavenly Father, thy will be done.*

Good Friends in High Places

I didn't expect my radiologist to become a good friend in a few minutes. But that is what happened. Turns out we have a lot in common: she remembers my son David from the high school basketball team. We share mutual friends and acquaintances. The radiologist has a daughter a year younger than David and a child at the university from which Andrew will graduate in the spring. We are at about the same life stage and both miss those school years when Ward and I followed basketball and she and her husband followed the chorus events that framed her daughter's high school life. I'm an RN and we both know many of the same people in the health care community. We even share a mutual friend who didn't beat breast cancer. And so, after the biopsy, she gave me her card with her home and cell phone numbers on it. "Call me any time you want to," she said.

I called her Sunday night and she talked with me for a long time, answering questions, helping me think out loud, offering her perspective on some of my thoughts. She helped me anticipate options which may be presented on Wednesday when I see the surgeon–and she gave me her stamp of approval when

I mentioned mastectomy. Furthermore, she gave me the names of several good plastic surgeons should I need reconstruction. I wonder if she knows what a blessing she is in my life. I don't know if I'll call her again, but I'm blessed to know that I can if I want to, and I'm confident that she will help me think clearly in the midst of a situation that can leave one a little addled! *Thank you, God, for putting your people in my life and navigating me to them in your perfect timing.*

January 13, Wednesday

Off to See the Wizard

I see the surgeon at 4:00 PM. The last several days have been such days of relief, but today the nausea returned, the anxious knots in my stomach dance–or struggle against one another, and my appetite has left me again. Ice cream might be palatable–it would slide down my throat and fill in the little crevices around the knots, but I'm not really in the mood for ice cream.

Tracy says I am amazing, and strong, and positive; and that's true, I am those things because that's how God made me. But I am also human, not quite fearful, but tense. Anxious to have answers, and yet holding back a bit of my emotional self in case the answers aren't the pleasant ones I want. Peace, people keep praying for me to have peace, and sending words to encourage me to rest in God's peace. I do have his peace, but I am also living Jesus' words "In this world, you will have trouble. But be of good cheer, I have overcome the world."[3] I am an overcomer because of what Christ has done for me, but I am walking in a land of trouble right now.

I feel like Dorothy–I'm off to see the wizard. Like her, I am eager to see him (the surgeon) and yet filled with dread as well.

---

3   *John 16:33*

But I don't want anyone to pull back the curtain and let me see his humanity. I want him to be bright, talented, intelligent, incredibly skilled, even gifted–a miracle worker in the hands of my living God. I want God to whisper to him: "I'm going to use you to heal Carolyn." Or even better, I dream of magical solutions "Mrs. Mustian, I just don't know how to explain it: the mass is completely gone." I'm praying for a very treatable mass, the good kind of bad cells, all neatly packaged in their little place.

Already I have women asking me questions–*nodule or duct involvement–what stage?* And I don't know the answers. One is better than the other, duct is good, I think. I suppose I feel I should know this, as an RN, but I spent my career at the veterans' hospital. Never saw a breast cancer case back then! I only treated two women in my years as an RN and we were challenged to meet their needs; one had MS and the other was a patient on the Substance Abuse Unit where I was head nurse. Today, when one walks through that veteran's medical center, there's a big sign that says "Women's Health"; an entire clinic dedicated to the care of women who have served in our branches of military. How far we have come! I hope it's true that we have come a long way in the treatment of breast cancer as well, and I hope I'm on the good end of the cancer scale.

This afternoon, I read the books the RN handed me last Friday when I got the biopsy results. I tucked them neatly into my purse and left them there, nearly forgotten until this afternoon when I sat down to fill out the paperwork to take to the breast surgeon's office. Then I sped read through the booklets, feeling no need to spend much time there. I don't have enough information yet to care which chemo treatments are described. I think I already know the surgery I want, but I must go with an open mind to listen to the wisdom of the doctor who specializes in the treatment of breast cancer.

One of the booklets said that one's survival rate is exactly the same for those who have a lumpectomy and those who have a mastectomy. But I'm not concerned with general survival rates; they deal in percentages. For those who succumbed to the disease, it was a 100% death rate, regardless of the surgery she had. I keep thinking of a relative who had prostate cancer. It spread. He died, way too young in my opinion at only 70 years old, I think. I remember his wife saying to me, "We chose not to have the surgery and now we don't know if we made the right choice. He might have made it if we'd had the surgery when this first started." I don't want to wonder if I would have made it had I not tried to hang on to my breasts.

My Aunt Lois' cancer moved from breast to breast bone, then lungs, and thus was her slow march to death. I think she survived nine years, and I will be grateful for nine years–much better than the months or year or so I might have had with melanoma. But I wonder if she had a lumpectomy first? I think I remember that they "got it all", but then it came back…so, I think I want these breasts gone. Less chance to harbor my potential killer.

Well, Ward just called. He's leaving work now. We're off to see the wizard. *Please, God, good news would be wonderful. But if that's not your plan for me, at least pour out your grace upon me, your amazing grace. And a big dose of courage would be nice as well.*

wednesday Night

You Want Courage?

After the appointment with the surgeon, Ward and I went straight to church for Wednesday night supper and Bible study. When I got home, I went to the computer to check my email, and this is one of the messages I found there, presented here exactly as Alice had emailed me:

Hi Carolyn,

Just a note to let you know I was thinking of you and praying for you today. I pray God will give you COURAGE, may His Word encourage you.

"Be strong and courageous. Do not be terrified; do not be discouraged, for the Lord your God will be with You wherever You go." Joshua 1:9

"In the day when I cried out, You answered me, and made me bold with strength in my soul." Psalm 138:3

"For I can do everything with the help of Christ who gives me the strength I need." Phil. 4:13

"Because the Sovereign Lord helps me, I will not be disgraced." Isaiah 50:7

Love in Christ,

Alice Kish

I am blown away by the words Alice has prayed for me, especially the word "courage" typed in big capital letters! *Thank you, God, for prayer warriors. Courage was exactly what I needed for this day. But you knew that already.*

I'm also thankful for the radiologist who makes herself so available to me. She is encouraging and eager to help. She offered to call Mark, a colleague of hers, to ask him about a particular doctor who had been recommended to me for reconstruction. They work in the same medical center. I gave her permission to tell Mark that I'm the patient. I first met

Mark when Ward and I moved into our first house in a new subdivision when we had only been married a year. Mark was just the eighth-grade whiz kid next door. Now he's a radiologist, head of the department at his hospital, I believe. At any rate, I am comforted that Mark will be able to answer my questions. It is a small world after all!

January 14, Thursday

The Gal with Cancer

Today has not been a very good day. I have felt like the girl with cancer. Yesterday I met with the surgeon. All the options were laid out for me surgically, and I basically needed to state my choice–double mastectomy is what I had planned on all along. I have had peace about my decision. And yet, when I had to speak the words out loud to the person who would actually make that happen, a bit of doubt crept in.

I called my radiology friend last night and thought I heard surprise in her voice when I told her my plans. She had readily agreed the previous week when I said mastectomy. She had said that would be her own choice. I think it was the "double" which took her by surprise. "Why are you considering a double?" she asked. I explained my thought process, and yet, I began to doubt myself. There are such momentous decisions to be made in such a short time–decisions which are irreversible and life changing. I need to get it right the first time, because there's no redo button on this merry-go-round.

Following the surgeon's office visit yesterday, Ward and I went straight to church for Wednesday night fellowship and there stood Alyse, as though God had placed her in just that spot for me to see her as I entered the fellowship hall for dinner.

Alyse is a three-year survivor. She sat with me through dinner and permitted me to pelt her with questions: practical ones about the surgery, recovery, and reconstruction. When I wondered what the scars would look like, she offered to let me see her scars if I wanted to. Sweet Alyse. I've always thought of her as quiet, a bit reserved, and yet she offered herself to me with candor, grace, and patient timing. She didn't overwhelm me with information for which I didn't ask. She just calmly spoke to my specific inquiries. I must remember to be an Alyse to the women God will put in my lane along this road. *Thank you, God, for sending Alyse to light my journey and pour peace along my pathway.*

She understood and validated my thought process. I watch her carefully now and see a woman who is living life fully. She sings in the choir, comes to church on Wednesday nights, too, and does all those things that a mother of a middle-school son does. She also offered this promise: "God will change you through all this, and it will be for the good. Not that you need changing," she was quick to add, perhaps fearing that she had implied there was something wrong with me. "I'm sure you are fine with God. But he changed me for the better through this."

"Oh, God still has plenty of work to do on me, Alyse," I laughingly assured her, "or I wouldn't still be here today." I believe that God doesn't leave us here on Earth when he has nothing else to accomplish in or through our lives. I know that God will use this experience to grow me in his spirit, and I pray that I will also be a blessing to others. *Dear God, please help me keep a teachable spirit through this process.* Alyse is the second woman to promise that God will bring good things out of this illness and recovery. *Here I am, God, make me useful in your kingdom.*

January 15, Friday

They're Not My Real Breasts

I have been amazed at the number of women, some casual acquaintances, but members of the sisterhood of breast cancer survivors, who have offered to whip open their blouses and show me their scars or their reconstructed bosoms. I haven't taken up any of their offers yet, but I went on line to do a little impersonal exploration. It doesn't look as tragic as I had feared, or as brutal. I suppose I have been envisioning the mastectomy scars women suffered 30 years ago when I was a nursing student. Surgery has come a long way for this disease.

Today, at the Butterfly lunch, my sweet friend Lisa, who just lost her sister to breast cancer, told about a neighbor opening her shirt to show her beautifully reconstructed breasts. I thought about whether I would be so bold, and then it hit me. They won't be my breasts. They will simply be fixtures on my chest, held in place by skin, which probably used to cover my midriff. It's the same skin that used to stretch nicely across my ribs and soak in sun when I wore my cute little white lacey two-piece bathing suit as a teenager many long years ago. Maybe they'll have fake nipples, all texturized by the skillful surgeon, or at least tattoos artfully drawn to resemble the real things. But it won't be the same as exposing breasts that had functions besides to fill out my blouse and keep my chest from caving in the wrong way.

I've even had breasts prostheses before, but they rested under the real things which still could theoretically function the way breasts are supposed to function. Never mind that at 60, I wasn't going to be feeding any babies; heck, I didn't feed them when I was 39. But they still had feeling and the other functions for which God made them.

Now, in mere weeks, the real things will be gone, partly dissected in some distant lab, then laid to rest wherever unneeded body parts go to repose–I don't think I want to know where that is, so if you know, please don't tell me. Some things are better left unsaid.

I will do my best to enjoy the new boobs. There's even some small joy in knowing I can get a set that fill my suits and blouses out completely. No more altering dresses and shirts to accommodate my rather small breasts. I'll be a little more of a Barbie® and a little less of a pear. That will be a novel experience–interior falsies that don't change size with my lifelong yo-yo dieting! *Lord God, help me keep my sense of humor on this roller coaster. Thank you that you made me more than just a pair of breasts. And when I'm on the other side of this journey next year, help my friends and acquaintances to forget that I am the woman who went through breast cancer. Help them to remember the woman I was and am–so much more than just a victim of cancer. Help them, and me, to see the many wonderful attributes you have built into my life which have little to do with what any of us look like, and everything to do with being the women we were created by you to be.*

"I Will Fear No Evil…"

As I talked with my sweet Butterflies today, six women who have gathered together to pray since my boys were little toddlers, I found myself trying to find the balance between hoping that this cancer would end and I could go on to a long and productive life, and yet, being realistic in acknowledging that cancer can crop up anywhere in the body–I've now experienced two different kinds within a few months of each other. There's a part of me that feels like a ticking time bomb, a dozen little terrorists cancer cells hiding along the roadside of my life, just waiting to blow up my nice little world.

It was in one of those moments when I had stopped talking and tried to listen to my friends that I heard the words of the

Psalmist whisper in my heart's ear…"Yeah, though I walk through the valley of the shadow of death, I will fear no evil, for thou art with me…"[4] The Good Shepherd holds my life in his hands. I can fear what tomorrow may bring, or I can enjoy the day he has given me, knowing that my fear cannot alter the plans my God has made for me. As Jesus reminded us in Matthew, "Can worry add one day to my life?"[5] No.

I hope the surgeon will get all the breast cancer. I hope the one who took the chunk of melanoma out of my arm last summer got it all before any errant cell escaped to hide and wait in some other unsuspecting organ of my anatomy. But if they didn't get every cell of cancer, I can't do anything about that. Only God knows if any will remain. Only God is truly capable of removing every cancerous cell from my body. Only God can keep additional new cancers from cropping up in the future. So I must make this phrase my watchword: "I will fear no evil, for thou art with me."

You Are Not Welcome…

My friend Martha penned an interesting card, dated 1-13-10. She wrote:

> *Kristin shared with me on Sunday about your recent breast cancer diagnosis. This is a sister-hood that does not welcome new members but I wanted you to know that I am praying for you…I love you and wish this had not come your way, but I will pray for you…"*

Yes, Martha, I would rather not have joined you in this sisterhood. It was not of my choosing, but I am here, and what a precious company of women surround me. Each of you embraces me with your hearts and your arms. Each of you

---

4   *Psalm 23 (KJV)*

5   *Matthew 6:27*

offers support: comfort, encouragement, prayers, hugs–and hope. Each of you write "Survivor" by your name and list a number and some of you have big numbers, even double digits!

I must learn, though, to be comfortable with the unknown. Those of us in this sisterhood are not really so different from the women who do not carry this mark of war waged against a vicious, subtle enemy. They also carry the threat of death in their lives, whether the threat is of illness, accident, the intentional cruel act of one human upon another, or simple old age. We are all marching towards our deaths. Some of us just have a clearer clue of which camouflage suit our enemy will likely wear. But all of us who carry the battle scars of cancer will not succumb to this particular combatant. Death wears many masks. Unless the Savior comes soon, each of us will do battle with death. But that will not be the end of us.

Some of us also wear the sign of the cross of Jesus, a reminder that we aren't defined by our cancer, even if it appears to win in the short term. And for those of us who know Jesus, our victory is already won because he has defeated death. While we do battle with this terrible cancerous enemy, some of the household of faith will meet Jesus at the hands of some other killer of the body. Sealed with the mark of God, though, we will be transformed from death to life in Christ. I must remember to carry myself well as a soldier of the Cross. After all, he has carried me well, lo, these many years. And he is up for the task of carrying me all the way home to him, whether I take that trip soon or later in my earthly trek.

And so, God, while Martha was not eager to welcome me into the sisterhood of cancer warriors, in fact we are both sisters in Christ and sisters in the common humanity which you have created. I am no different this month than I was last except I am now aware of the next few steps of my journey, which you are constantly unveiling. Unless you have another unexpected twist in my immediate pathway, I know I will submit to a doctor's knife shortly and have the landscape of my chest forever altered.

But if I didn't take his skilled scalpel to my breasts, my body still would have been greatly altered by disease. My path you set before I ever breathed a breath. Help me live worthy of your call, Sweet Jesus. Let me walk bravely in this place you have put me. You must have a good reason for this part of my journey, for I believe that nothing is wasted in your economy, God. Let me not squander this time. After all, haven't I been praying about what I'm supposed to do next in this world? And to think last summer I thought it was a job at the VA! Thank you, Lord, for at least giving me a good run at that job. I know I would have been good at it–help me be good at this one to which I've now been assigned. I love you, Lord.

Aunt Lois

My dad's oldest sister died of breast cancer a few years ago. I asked him about the course of her disease recently. He said they removed her breast and when it had healed, she came to Virginia to visit him. While here, she found another lump beside the surgical site. So she returned to South Carolina for more surgery, then no treatment following surgery, according to my dad's understanding. Then more cancer cropped up and eventually she died.

I don't know if my dad has the story right, but he expressed a lot of frustration that the doctors had failed to treat her properly at the beginning. How do we know they didn't treat her right? How do we know she didn't get any treatment? Aunt Lois is a pretty quiet person. Then again, my surgeon said I might not need chemo after surgery either. I'll surely get a second opinion on that one. Perhaps I'll call my cousin Irene to see what she knows about her mother's course of treatment. Now that I think about it, I may have a picture of Aunt Lois in a wig. That would certainly indicate chemo. I'll make that phone call soon; I want answers.

January 20, Wednesday

Labels

I'm afraid I've lost my identity as a person. Going to church on Sunday was a painful experience. I just wanted to slip in unnoticed, go to my seat, and find some sort of normalcy. Ward dropped me and Andrew off at the front door while he went to park the car. I smiled, spoke, and rushed by people as quickly as I could. But in the sanctuary a couple of men jumped up and hugged me in big bear hugs, expressing their sorrow, sympathy, and promises of prayers. At the end of the service, other people also rushed up to offer their condolences at my misfortune. And I appreciate every warm thought, every attempt to offer encouragement, comfort, prayer support–but I'm not handling this role of sick person, marked woman, very well. I wish I could get back to normal, boring Carolyn.

I suppose I thought that since my diagnosis was out of the closet the previous Sunday, I could somehow slip back into being just Carolyn, but that wasn't to be. Even folks who wrote emails, made phone calls, or sent cards and notes felt the need to once again speak to me in person about the *big C*. Fortunately, those precious women in the Cancer Survivor Sisterhood knew to simply smile and say hello.

I had to laugh when we got home, because I was expressing my frustration with my inability to be anonymous. Andrew said, "I know, Mom. I thought if one more guy jumped up and hugged you, I was going to have to start bouncing 'em!" Well said, Andrew! Spoken as only my precious college man could speak.

In fact, I was immediately taken back to another time, another place when my protective eldest son tried to defend me. We were at a fundraiser dinner for an organization in which Ward served as a board member. He had stepped away from the table and I was sitting there with Andrew, about 8, and Dave, one year younger. One of Ward's friends came up, greeted me and kissed me hello. Andrew swelled up like an angry blowtoad. When Ward came back to the table, Andrew reported what he had witnessed, concluding with "Dad, he kissed her!"

"That's OK, Andrew," Ward replied, "he's just being friendly."

"NO, Dad! He kissed her on the lips!" Andrew exclaimed, indignant and red-faced. I knew at that moment I would always have a protector and defender in this son!

Labels have always scared me because they cause people to make assumptions and focus on the surface, rather than the person inside the skin. For those reasons, I have always been pretty private about my health issues and some of my personal history as well. I share very little about my past, preferring to be judged by my current successes and failures, rather than those I have lived beyond! And God knows, I have enough current stuff without digging up old wounds and weaknesses.

I was sad most of Sunday, grieving for what has been lost with this diagnosis, still very much aware that it could be worse, but sad all the same. I suppose a therapist would suggest that I am moving through the stages of grieving, and I cannot argue with that. In fact, yesterday as I filled out yet another medical form, I neglected to list either the melanoma or the breast cancer on my history form–the denial stage, no doubt. And no doubt also a reflection of my unwillingness to accept this current label thrust upon me. Oh, the challenges of adjusting to a label not of my choosing. I'll be much better off if I can transform this disease into a mark of ownership of Christ. When I talked about seals last fall as I taught Revelation to the precious Powhatan ladies, I did not envision God marking me with this particular style of seal.

*Lord, at the conclusion of this challenge, find me worthy to wear
your seal, in whatever form this cross will take.*

Monday morning was still a blue morning until Pat Rudd called.
Pat, my sweet, sweet friend. Pat, who suffered with me through
nursing school, came to work with me at the Veterans Hospital
a few months after graduation, only to have me leave the unit
within weeks to accept a head nurse job on another unit. Dear
Pat, we can go for months without seeing one another, but our
connection is strong and sure because at the base of it, we share
the sisterhood of Jesus.

Besides, we are disaster nurses, and not the kind one might
think! We met the first week of nursing school. Both of us lived
off campus and thus we were called "commuters". The Associate
Dean came into the student lounge and asked us commuters
to find a partner to share a locker. One of us was carrying a big
Bible, we don't remember which one, but we zeroed in on each
other, became locker buddies and soon partners for whatever
else required a two-some. Within a month, that included
"Foundations Lab" where we learned to give injections, make
beds hospital style, take vital signs, and give bed baths. That
was an adventure in disaster! I've always run a low temperature:
97 and some change, as opposed to the standard 98.6 F. So
when Pat did my vitals and reported my temperature as 98.6, I
momentarily got a surprised look on my face. But the look in her
eyes warned me not to say a word, so I resisted the temptation to
comment. The instructor checked her off as competent, and she
later whispered to me, "I forgot to shake the mercury down–that's
why your temperature was high." We giggled and moved on.

Sometime later, we had to give one another bed baths. Each
of us lived through that, checked off successfully, and then
prepared to go to the next class. I stood with Pat behind the
protective curtain, underclothes in hand as she picked up the
basin of water, tripped and spilled it all over my bra and panties.

We giggled again; I wrung out my clothes as best I could and sat through the next lecture in damp garb.

But these two little incidents were pretty harmless compared to what I did to Pat. When it came time to practice injections, we started with an orange, and then progressed to giving our lab partners saline injections. Pat did a great job on me. Now it was my turn to give an injection in her buttock. Back in those days, injections were given by "throwing" the needle, dart-like, while still holding it in one's hand. I suppose the theory was that it was less painful to go in fast. But poor Pat, when I threw the needle, she flinched. Startled, I let go and the needle momentarily hung there unsupported in her body swaying back and forth like a bad cartoon! Somehow, though, we both passed Foundations of Nursing and moved on to more challenging adventures.

Fast forward to our senior year. One day we sat down for a Community Health lecture, looked up and saw that the topic was "Disaster Nurses" and immediately burst into laughter. "Disaster Nurses! That's us!" we both exclaimed simultaneously. Of course the lecture was about delivering nursing care in massive natural or manmade disasters, but to this day we laugh about being disaster nurses. Pat went on to develop an amazing career in nursing, but I bailed: first to hospital administration, and later to full-time mom.

And then on Monday, when I really needed a friend, Pat called and said, "I'm off today, Carolyn. Do you need someone to go with you to any appointments, or come over, or go to lunch? You name it, and I'll be there." I decided to do my plastics consultation alone, but Pat met me at the house afterwards. In fact, she was there when I pulled in the driveway. Irony of ironies, as the cancer victim (me) bounced out of her car, Pat the nurse who had come to minister to me, slowly and gingerly eased herself out of her cute little sports car and crept up the driveway.

"What happened to you?" I asked.

"I pulled a muscle after I talked to you."

Dear friend that she is, Pat stayed all afternoon, sat in straight back chairs, warmed her aching muscles before the fire, listened to my ramblings and spoke to the emotions that rollercoastered through my heart.

Pat assured me I am normal–well, at least what's normal for me! She helped me think through treatment options one more time and sort through my conflicted feelings. She gave me permission to be frustrated with my situation and reminded me that I do not walk alone. Not that I've felt alone, but it can be lonely in the midst of a crowd, and right now, I feel a little lonely and unsure of myself or my future. And impatient. I've always had a plan, and now, I have precious few options. I am reminded of Jesus' words to Peter after the resurrection, "…When you were younger you dressed yourself and went where you wanted; but when you are old, you will stretch out your hands and someone else will dress you and lead you where you do not want to go."[6] Lord, I'm not much liking the place I am heading at this moment, and I don't think I'm old, and I want to cry out "I'm no Peter." But I hear the still small voice of God which says, "Your call is the same as his: Follow me." *And I will, Lord. Help me follow faithfully.*

Don't Say "Breast Cancer" to Your Hair Dresser

I have been letting my hair grow longer the last several months, but after I got the breast cancer diagnosis, I knew I would be facing some time of not being able to use the hair curlers or curling iron or any of those devices I use to keep from looking scraggly. Furthermore, I still don't know if I'll face a course of chemo, which could mean no hair for a while.

---

6   John 21:18

The day after my diagnosis, I went to my hairdresser for a light trim. I explained to her that I'm trying to let my hair grow out, but will be facing surgery soon and maybe chemo, so I wanted a cut that is easy to manage with a simple shampoo and dry. I also rambled that in spite of my efforts to grow my hair longer, before it's all over, I might have to resort to a short cut. But I think I neglected to emphasize that, at this point, I still wanted my hair to grow to all one length. I know I said I wanted to keep it long, but I'm pretty sure after I said "Breast Cancer" I either failed to communicate clearly or she failed to grasp the little details of the style I wanted.

Regardless of who dropped the ball, we had a failure to communicate and by the time I had slept on it overnight, I suspected I was in trouble. It stuck out in weird places. I spent the week trying various ways to shape a pretty style, but to no avail. There were way too many layers for my already fine hair. I went back this past Saturday, explained more clearly that I'm trying for all one length, had a lot cut off the bottom and am now hoping that when my sweet husband has to blow dry my hair, he will be able to somehow make me look half-way presentable. He has great dexterity with tiny little tools in people's mouths, but I'm not so confident about how he'll wield a hair dryer or curling iron.

The short lesson of this escapade, though, is this: don't say "Breast Cancer" to your hairdresser until after the haircut is complete. That term becomes a big scary ball in the middle of the floor that expands and gobbles up any words that come after it, like a giant PacMan® gone crazy! I learned a good lesson, because when I went to my nail tech the next week, I didn't say a word about my diagnosis. I'll just disappear for a month or so for surgery and when I come back, she'll probably have to put a fresh set of nails on my fingers.

But there's a bigger lesson in this, too. Once upon a time, I would have been frustrated or maybe even cried that I had to cut off a couple of inches of hair. Not now. It will grow back. I'm about to have a couple of breasts cut off and I'll never get them back. What a different perspective a few weeks can make.

Right now, I'm just hoping I'll get to keep some of my lymph nodes. The radiologist said yesterday that one is abnormal. It could be cancer or it could be inflammatory response to the biopsy. Worst-case scenario, the surgeon has to take all the lymph nodes and I'll be left with an arm that swells for the rest of my life. Oh, that and metastatic cancer. *Please Lord, could I skip that one?*

Calendars, Emails

Boy has my calendar changed. It used to hang on the wall half-forgotten or occasionally used to note fun things or dates I was going to help my niece with babysitting. Now I drag it from room to room, near whichever phone I might use next. It's a conglomerate of doctor appointments, medical tests, and phone numbers and driving directions to folks I've consulted about this disease.

For the last several Christmases, Andrew has given me a personalized calendar. It is filled with family pictures featuring my precious boys and the children and grandchildren of my heart (my sister's children and grandchildren). This year, inexplicably, he ordered a size larger than he normally selects. It was too big to hang in any of the usual places, so I cleared a spot in the laundry room. He thought he had made a mistake in size, but of course that turns out not to be the case. I need all of that space to write appointments and keep notes. It's packed with info, and its only January!

It looks like an old lady's calendar. I've entered my parents' generation's style of living. Their social life consists of appointments with various health care givers, interspersed with funeral home visits and funerals. I'm not doing the funeral home circuit yet, and I'm hoping I'm not going to end up on someone else's funeral circuit any time soon, but the possibility is there. I read a book once which described old age as beginning when one's health starts to fail. I really figured I had another 20 years or so before that milestone– and maybe I do! But I'm not as confident of that longevity now as I once was. I felt so safe because I was in good health–no heart disease, a little overweight, but not too worried about that except for looks. After all, none of my large relatives had heart disease or stroke until well into their 80s.

Furthermore, I can out-work, out-walk, out-shop, and out-sightsee folks twenty to forty years younger than me. When my family visited DC last spring break, it was my 20-something sons who were ready to call it quits both Saturday night and Sunday afternoon while I still had places to see and things to do. I'm the woman in the family who can upholster sofas, sew and hang floor length drapes, move furniture and most anything else I want to unless I want to feign helplessness to get the boys involved in my projects.

Healthy relatives, healthy me, lots of energy–I thought I was home free. I neglected to note, until several months ago, that my father's side of the family had begun to succumb to cancer in various varieties. I'm starting to think that my gene pool is not as great as I once believed.

Exercise, Genes, and Breast Cancer

Speaking of health and gene pools, the latest research suggests that women who exercise at least an hour a day have a significantly lower risk of developing breast cancer or experiencing recurrence once they have had it. My son, who is just completing an undergrad degree in biology, says it's all about genes. Unfortunately, I hate to exercise! And

I'm suspicious of studies, especially those which speak about obesity, exercise, and whatever is considered "healthy eating"– which changes with predictable frequency. Suppose the cancer gene is connected to the "hate exercise" gene and it just so happens that people who like to exercise also don't carry the cancer gene? Who knows, that could be the case? We don't know!

Anyway, I expect that after this bout is over, I'll try once again for the millionth time to start an exercise program. It will last about a week, if I'm lucky, and then I'll be sick of sweating (which I also hate), and spending all that time walking when I could be doing a nice craft project, or writing a lecture, or typing a journal. Or maybe I can do some research on that hate-exercise-cancer gene connection, which I'm sure is there–those researchers just aren't looking in the right place. *And anyway God, couldn't you keep me from getting breast cancer if you wanted to, even if I don't exercise? And won't it come back if that's your plan, even if I do exercise? I know this sounds like circular reasoning, but God, this thing's got my head dizzy! Could you at least stop the brain spin? Thank you.*

And while you're at it, Lord, would you please cause me to make the right medical choices, and direct my doctors in the right pathways, too, in spite of ourselves? There's so much cancer treatment research out there and it is often conflicting. What's a girl supposed to do? You are aware of the many medical choices people have made based upon the most up-to-date research, only to learn a year or so later that it was wrong. So would you please direct my medical path? I need you to be the lamp to my feet–and the surgeon's brain and hands. Thank you again.

Thank You, God, for Women!

Thank you, God, for women: smart, kind, encouraging women who speak words of life and blessing to me. Today I saw my dermatologist for my routine six-month body check (which people with skin cancer usually get). When I told her about my new diagnosis of breast cancer and my decision for a double mastectomy, she agreed with me completely. She said that would be her choice as well, and she is much younger and much more beautiful than me. She is also way smarter–an Ivy League graduate who also taught there, she is nevertheless a young woman, mom of little children, preschoolers, I think. Yet she said faced with a similar diagnosis, she would choose the same path, and even have a hysterectomy if it was indicated. Then she smiled and said, "Besides they can make some beautiful breasts and they'll stay perky." Perky breasts are no small thing for a woman entering her sixties!

And God, I so needed another confirmation that I am doing the right thing. I feel like you sent her to answer my prayer to you earlier today to help me and my doctors make the right decisions. She said she will pray for me and I know that she will. Thank, you God, that you have surrounded me front and back and on all sides with your precious children.

The dermatologist and I also talked about breast cancer and the statistics about exercise, etc. She said, "Well, yes, everyone knows exercise is good for you and eating lots of veggies is healthy. But who can live like that all the time? Besides, breast cancer strikes one in ten women. One in ten! That's just life–it happens to lots of people and they didn't do anything to cause it. There's such a tendency to try to blame the patient, but these things just happen." *Dear God, thank you for using this compassionate dermatologist as your mouthpiece and blessing to me today.*

I will stop second-guessing myself and my decisions now. I will stop beating myself up for getting breast cancer. As Andrew said, "It's just genetics, Mom, it's just genetics." Yes, Andrew, it is genetics in a fallen world.

My surgeon called me as I was on my way to the dermatologist to tell me that the MRI was fine. I mentioned that Mark said one of the lymph nodes appeared to be enlarged and he agreed but said that was not all that unusual, often the result of the biopsy, just as Mark had told me. In addition, he said the surgery would take care of it. I'm an RN and a little knowledge can be a dangerous thing. I'm relieved to hear my surgeon minimize the risks, but I know that it could be trouble-anything is possible. Nevertheless, I'm going to focus upon the doctor's upbeat phone call and remind myself it's all up to God to set the course of this disease. And I'm thankful God has trained up some very competent doctors in every field. I'm also trusting God to lead me to them.

Alyse and Martha both sought me out tonight at church. I continue to be thankful for this precious sisterhood: women drawn together by a nasty disease but committed to be encouragers, comforters, cheerleaders for one another. When those who know me casually say, "Wow, you're handling this so well…" I can look at them and say, "Yes, but I have my moments!" Those who have walked this road smile knowingly and say, "Oh, yes, we understand, and sometimes we still have our moments!"

Cancer can become the threatening shadow that hangs over the sisterhood of the pink ribbon; yet the truth is that the threat of death hangs over each of us daily. It behooves us, therefore, to live each day like it was our last as we plan to live like we have 100 years before us. After all, when the sisters of the pink ribbon also belong to the household of faith, we have eternity spread before us like a feast. It's just the temporary separation from those we love on Earth, which rattles our cage and awakes the grieving monster who would steal our joy of the moment. *Oh, God, keep the monsters at bay!*

January 21, Thursday

Doctors Can Build a Boob–But Not a Brain

Ward's cousin called last night to check on me and of course I asked about her niece who is battling cancer, which attacked her spine and now threatens her brain. She is a young college girl, an incredibly gifted writer on a full scholarship. She should be enjoying college and making plans for postgraduate work or a career. Instead this brave young woman is deciding cancer treatment options. She must choose between radiation, which could rob her of her intelligence or even of herself entirely, and an experimental drug which, if it works, would deny the cancer its blood supply and hopefully save her life. *Oh, God, would you please touch those crazy cancer cells and set this precious young woman free from the ravages of this terrible disease. You are the God of life and hope and I pray for her Jeremiah 29:11. Please give her hope and a future, please!*

When I finished talking with Ward's cousin, I was struck by my blessing: Doctors can build a boob, but not a brain. I can live a very normal life with the breast-like objects the doctor will create for me, but the college girl needs her brain in all the wonderful form it has just as God created it. We each get one brain and there is nothing which can substitute for a healthy, whole one. Skilled doctors will work their creative genius on my body and their artistic ministry to me will permit me to masquerade as whole. *But dear God, only you can make a brain. Please work your creative, marvelous genius on this sweet young woman battling brain cancer. Give her life and grace and healing in the ways that only you can do.*

I am struck by how profane cancer is. It's a destroyer that wreaks havoc on God's marvelous creation. And yet, God is the redeemer of all things. He redeems our lives, our times, our troubles, our pain, our joys, our souls. *For whatever pathways you have planned for the co-ed and me, God grant us grace and strength, peace and courage, and comfort for those who love us should our pathways take us through the valley of the shadow of death.* A lump gathers in my throat as I write these words, but my mind screams: focus, focus, focus on God. *Make my pathways straight according to your perfect plan, precious Jesus. Make my pathways straight.*

I read back over these words, Lord, and they sound like the cry of a teenage drama queen and we both know I'm well past seventeen! So let me try once more: Make me real, Lord, like the Velveteen Rabbit: Make me real.

I remember the first time I heard of the Velveteen Rabbit. I was a college girl myself, in the school of nursing at the university. I was also a leader in the Christian fellowship there, which met in the women's dormitory. On any given Sunday evening, we would have about a hundred folks gathered in the lobby, praising God in song and message. One Sunday night, I was the speaker. My friend, Cesie, introduced me with this passage from the Velveteen Rabbit:

"What is REAL?" asked the Rabbit one day, when they were lying side by side near the nursery fender, before Nana came to tidy the room. "Does it mean having things that buzz inside you and a stick-out handle?"

"Real isn't how you are made," said the Skin Horse. "It's a thing that happens to you. When a child loves you for a long, long time, not just to play with, but REALLY loves you, then you become Real."

"Does it hurt?" asked the Rabbit.

"Sometimes," said the Skin Horse, for he was always truthful. "When you are Real you don't mind being hurt."

"Does it happen all at once, like being wound up," he asked, "or bit by bit?"

"It doesn't happen all at once," said the Skin Horse. "You become. It takes a long time. That's why it doesn't happen often to people who break easily, or have sharp edges, or who have to be carefully kept. Generally, by the time you are Real, most of your hair has been loved off, and your eyes drop out and you get loose in the joints and very shabby. But these things don't matter at all, because once you are Real you can't be ugly, except to people who don't understand." [7]

As she began to read the words, I thought, "That's not very flattering!" But as the passage continued, I realized she was paying me a high compliment. She concluded by saying I was a real, genuine person. I promptly went out and purchased a copy of the book and made it my goal to be real. I think I'm about to be more beat up and wear-worn than the Velveteen Rabbit ever dreamed of being, and I must think of the bruises and bandages as badges of love because I know that I am greatly loved by many people–and by God. And he is making me real.

The Burden of Perceptions

In fact, being real has its challenges. I carry myself with dignity. I don't want to kick against the goads of life. I want to be a reflection of my Savior who gives me grace and courage for this journey. He has also given me a fair share of humor and blessed me with a positive attitude. But I am these things because of him–the way he made me and the ways he is equipping me for each moment.

Not that I don't have my sad times, my moments of anxiety, my moments of wondering how this will all turn out. And I really don't know. I don't know if I'll be a cancer survivor or a cancer

7 Williams, Margery: *The Velveteen Rabbit*. Doubleday, 1922.

victim. But either way, I want to be God's woman in this place. I want to live in such a way that those who watch will see Jesus walking by my side, and carrying me when I can no longer carry my body on my own two legs.

Herein is the rub: I want to be God's honest woman. I want to be the reflection of my Savior. So far, I'm not acting. Folks say, "You are so brave, you are so strong, you are so positive." I am those things by the grace of God. But already on this short trip, people have seen me sad and glad. They've seen me weak and strong–and will see me looking worse before I look better. *Help them remember both sides of my experience, Lord.* I'm not looking to be someone's hero–I just want to be God's woman.

So in spite of my emotions or moods of the moment, please Jesus, let them see you in my life. In the midst of this firestorm, let them see you beside me just like you stood beside Daniel's friends. Astonish the onlookers, Lord, because you enable your own to walk through the fires of life and not have soot and ashes or the smell of smoke on the other side.

And while we're thinking about the book of Daniel, Lord, you know how I love big cats. I'd be delighted if you turned some of the roaring lions of my life into the tame majestic cats who surrounded Daniel in their den. Seal the mouth of the cancer and cause it to lay down like a house kitten, and then Lord, if you would just remove it to the place where it can do no more harm, I'd be very grateful. If you would banish the sleeping cancer kitten to some distant barn, that would be fine by me. A barn far away in some desolate place would be great, where it can't hurt anyone else either. But regardless of what you decide to do, Lord, let Jesus shine through all of this.

Dental School

A scarce two months ago, I was storming heaven's gates with prayers that Andrew would get into dental school. Now I'm hoping God didn't keep him out so he could help me die. When I mentioned that to Ward, he pooh-poohed the notion immediately, probably because he's afraid to even let his mind go in that direction. But I must be honest with myself: I don't have a clue what God is about to do. I only know that life often takes an unexpected turn, and not necessarily in the direction I think it should go. In fact, life frequently doesn't take the turn I expected! At those times, and now, I'm left to teeter on the brink, wanting to believe that God will heal me, but knowing that his ways are not the ways of man.

I resist the temptation to say, "God, if he gets into dental school this year, I will know that I'm going to live, but if he doesn't, then I must be terminal." Of course that ignores a third option: I will die and he will go to dental school this year. I learned a long time ago that when I can only see two options, or even three or more, God usually has another up his sleeve that I didn't envision. It is my job to keep alert to his leadership, rest in his presence, and follow in his footsteps, wherever those steps may lead.

After that first frightening week when I was pretty sure I was dying of metastatic melanoma, then learned it was breast cancer instead, I've felt very upbeat, jubilant even that I didn't get an immediate death sentence. But I haven't exactly gotten a promise of long life or complete cure, either. Come to think of it, neither does anyone else. We're all terminal. We just deceive ourselves with thinking we will live well and healthy to a ripe old age of eighty, or ninety or more. We are so foolish to think we can exercise enough, or eat healthy enough, or avoid danger successfully enough to guarantee long life. We cannot. Our days are written in God's Book of Life, and I must keep reminding myself that he will keep me here for exactly the time he allotted to me before I was ever born[8]. I keep forgetting that. And Andrew will get into dental school–or not–exactly on the

---

8   *Psalm 139*

schedule God has planned for him. Our challenge is to live fully and faithfully each day as we move toward the goal God has set before us both.

January 22, Friday

Camisoles and Other Clothes

Nancy, dear Nancy. She met me for coffee this morning bearing gifts. I was surprised, although knowing Nancy as I do, I should have anticipated that she would not arrive at Starbucks® empty-handed. And what was in the pink gift bag? A Kim Newlen camisole–the one Kim designed following her own dance with cancer. It's called "Look Better Than You Feel"®[9] and it has pockets for foam padding and the dreaded drains which will hang out of my body for a couple of weeks post-op. There was also a book in the bag: "Praying through Cancer".[10] It is a collection of devotionals written by godly women who have battled cancer in its various forms. And finally, a chocolate foil wrapped heart that said "I'm yours", delivering Kim's message: "I'm here for you." And I know that she is.

Kim and I met years ago when we served together in CBS. I was the mother of two small boys and Kim had a lovely little daughter. We were sisters in Christ, and now also sisters of the pink ribbon society. God has used Kim mightily to bless women through her **"Sweet Monday"**®[11] ministry, which extends around the world. When she became a breast cancer survivor herself, she opened wide her arms (well, maybe not wide at first!) to embrace those women who also face breast cancer. Interesting that Nancy mentioned Kim lives with a swollen arm because her lymph nodes were removed, and that's the issue

---

9   *www.LookBetterThanYouFeel.com*

10   *Praying Through Cancer: Set Yourself Free From Fear, by Susan Sorensen and Laura Geist, W Publishing, 2006.*

11   *www.SweetMonday.org*

that troubles me at this moment. But Kim survives with this malady, and I can, too, if that's the direction this disease takes in my body. *But if it's all the same to you, Lord, I'd like to pass on that dish: No thank you, I don't care for any swollen arms right now.*

Nancy selected just the right camisole for me: a wild black and white zebra print. I love animals and snappy clothes and this camisole will get its share of wear. I'll smile when I put it on and resist the temptation to mourn my missing body parts. I'll celebrate that I know the designer personally and relax knowing that Kim's and Nancy's love also hugs my body like the lovely camisole I wear. Holding all of me in place will be the love of Christ–the designer of my life and soul–I know that Designer, too. He is not surprised by this turn in life, and has already prepared many warm arms and open hearts to hold me tight (but not too tight at first!) *Thank you, God, for wrapping me in love.*

Vitamins and Emails and Magic Mushrooms

Almost as soon as the word of my cancer diagnosis got out, I began to get phone calls and emails and magazine articles reporting amazing and sometimes offbeat cures for cancer. I got email prayer chains entitled, "Pass this on to everyone you know and pray for a cure for Breast Cancer…." Do people have these emails sitting in their email file, just waiting to hear of a new diagnosis? If it had been heart disease or stroke, would they have shuffled through and found an email prayer for that?

There were food cures, reports of amazing diets and vitamins and foods with magical healing powers. *Oh, God, I'd really like to take a magic mushroom and be well.* But I don't have time to experiment on myself that way. This growth must come out of my body now. I hope that in a few years, they will have a pill or potion one can swallow and have the cancer shrivel up and die. But I can't bet on someone else's hunch right now.

I know my friends mean well. They bring these odd pieces of information as their desperate offering of help. We all grasp for cures for those we love. We are all looking for the magic mushroom, the special asparagus, the just-right prayer with power to heal, the miraculous food to restore our health, our youth, my boobs. *At the end of the day, Lord God, you are sovereign. You will heal me or not according to your perfect plan. I will trust you to direct me in the right course of medical treatment, lead me to the one who has healing in his hands in whatever form that takes, and intervene if I make the wrong choice. Because you, O God, are able to do far and beyond all that we could ask or dream. You know our needs before they are spoken. You know the needs I don't even know to ask. Keep me centered on you, Lord; keep me centered on you, and I will have all that I need for health and life, whatever form that takes.*

Acts of Love and Blessing

Since my little pity party last Sunday, when I was already weary of my new title of "Gal with Cancer" I have made a major attitude adjustment. I know that people are trying to be kind. They want to be encouragers. They are searching for ways to reach out to me–this is new territory for them, too. Sometimes they are awkward, sometimes they are at a loss–but always they are trying to minister and love and serve in the best way they know how. And sometimes I am awkward, too. I must not expect them to read my emotions or my needs; I'm not always sure of them myself.

I keep remembering my two years of pregnancy. It was sort of like being an elephant; they carry their unborn babies for two years. I was pregnant for two years with barely a five month space between the two pregnancies. I remember my frustration with people, male and female, strangers or casual acquaintances, who would reach out and pat my stomach. I felt so violated. My personal space was breeched, and I hated it. Then one day, my dear friend, Nancy Taylor, shared her approach to these gestures. She said she had originally experienced my same feelings that people were touching inappropriately. But she finally realized they were trying to reach lovingly toward the baby she carried. I never got accustomed to those personal touches. I did learn to interpret them not as a personal assault, but rather as an act of affection directed toward my preborn child.

Now I remind myself that people are struggling for ways to express love and encouragement to me in a situation which is frightening to them, a reminder of all our vulnerability and the fragileness of life. Sometimes they ask way too many questions about the cancer, how I found it, how it will be treated. They want to know my prognosis. I don't even know my prognosis—how can I tell them? Yet I think they ask for a prognosis, looking for me to assure them I will be cured because they want to celebrate life with me. I want to offer them hope; I want hope myself. Nevertheless, my hope is anchored in Christ regardless of the prognosis. We're all terminal anyway.

I'm also not thrilled about saying "double mastectomy" even though I am confident that this is the best course for me. But it's a little off putting to know that for the rest of my life, when people look at me they may be thinking, "There's Carolyn with no breasts. I wonder what those fake ones look like under her shirt?" I must remember to think of my scars as the battle scars of life, symbols of a life well lived in the care of a Savior who stood beside me on a broken planet where genes are flawed and germs are gone awry.

I am so Blessed!

I must remind myself that I've been blessed beyond all I once dared hope or dream. I didn't start adult life with a very good beginning. I married young, way too young, and found myself divorced while still a teen. It was a terrible way to begin and I continued to make bad choices when it came to men. Then one day at twenty-five, I met The Man from Galilee, and he has made all the difference in my life. He has transformed my life, just as he said he would.

Today, I can celebrate with joy the blessings God has poured into my life: Ward, wonderful Ward, who has loved me with all my flaws. Ward, who will still love me when I am the Boobless Wonder! My precious sons, Andrew and David, born late in my life against the odds of endometriosis, an absent ovary, and organs oddly shaped because I was a DES[12] baby. God, giver of life, gave me two precious sons, and I am doubly blessed because I got to raise them to adulthood. Not every mother gets that chance, but this privilege has been mine. Once upon a time, I read the words of the prophet Isaiah:

> *"Sing, O barren woman, you who never bore a child; burst into song, shout for joy, you who were never in labor; because more are the children of the desolate woman than of her who has a husband," says the LORD. "Enlarge the place of your tent, stretch your tent curtains wide, do not hold back; lengthen your cords, strengthen your stakes. For you will spread out to the right and to the left; your descendants will dispossess nations and settle in their desolate cities."[13]*

I claimed it for my verse. Marriage once looked remotely possible and I thought that spiritual children would be my legacy. I expanded my tents, shared the good news of Jesus Christ with whoever would listen. Then in my mid-thirties, God surprised me with Ward, followed by two precious sons.

---

12   *DES is an abbreviation for a hormonal drug which was given to pregnant women in the late 1940's and 1950's to prevent miscarriages. Years later scientists discovered that it had caused birth defects in the reproductive organs of some women exposed to the drug in utero*

13   *Isaiah 53:1-3*

But God also expanded the tents of my heart to encircle my sister's teens when she died suddenly at 39. I call her son and daughter the children of my heart and celebrate their children as heart-grandchildren as though they were my own.

God's blessings don't stop there. I do have spiritual children: those who came to Christ because he let me tell his Gospel story. And sisters and brothers galore: people of faith who call God "Father" and celebrate salvation through Jesus, our Redeemer. They are my prayer team now, the ones who will hold me up to heaven when the burden down here seems too heavy. They are my encouragers who will bring meals and sit with me through the long days of recovery. *Lord God, you expanded my tents well beyond the boundaries I thought were my limits. You are so generous, Heavenly Father!*

January 24, Sunday

Pregnancy and Cancer: Distant Cousins

I keep bumping into people and thoughts and experiences that carry me back to the days of my pregnancies. Perhaps that is because those two nine month adventures are the only other times in my life where I felt handicapped and physically confined for any length of time. There were also foreign objects growing in my body then, but the babies who eventually came out were much more welcome than these nasty cancer cells. Although come to think of it, those babies altered the landscape of my body, too. I'm still carrying baby fat, and they are 21 and 22! Or, at least that's my excuse for not being a size six!

Pregnancy may have been easier had I been 10 or 15 years younger when I started that journey, but I was not. I was on the downside of 37 when Andrew was born, and nearly 39 when David arrived. I was thrilled and blessed beyond measure in both pregnancies, but it's not easy being old and pregnant. My chart with my first pregnancy said "elderly prima gravid", a medical term which means old for a first pregnancy, and had I not been a nurse I might have been insulted to be labeled elderly!

My boss, a physician about my age, or maybe a little younger, was a single man who was exceedingly kind and compassionate towards me. I remember one particularly challenging day, I drug my weary self into his office, plopped down in a chair and said, "Bob, I don't care what they taught you in medical school, the truth is that pregnancy is a severe handicap and there is nothing, **nothing** normal about it! Nothing in my body works like it's supposed to, and all those women who claim they never felt better in their lives are liars! This is a miserable, debilitating condition and I can't wait for this baby to get here so my body can start functioning normally again. I just want to feel good, and be able to live my life like a normal woman." Bless Bob's heart, he just listened and empathized with me. Of course the up side of that adventure was that I delivered a healthy bouncing baby boy, all 8 pounds of him and within a few weeks my body was back to normal. Within a few months I was pregnant with my second son. As I moved into the role of mother, then pregnant mother, my life developed a new kind of normal. In the ensuing years, however, I learned that Christian author Patsy Clairmont is right: "Normal is Just a Setting on Your Dryer"[14]

Now I am in a battle for my life. In ten days, I will submit myself to a surgeon's knife, but there will be no more normal for me as I currently define normal. At the end of the procedure,

---

[14]   *Clairmont, Patsy: Normal is Just a Setting on Your Dryer! (September 1999)*

I will have less and not more. No cancer cells, hopefully, but no real breasts either. If all goes well, in a few months I will be well healed from the mastectomy and continuing with the reconstructive process. In about a year, I will be a sixty-one year old woman with the perky implants of a twenty-something. I hope I will still have my sense of humor.

But from now on, "well" will have a different definition for me. I will probably live the rest of my life wondering if the cancer is coming back, or if another form is lurking just beneath the shaky surface of my life. I will cling tightly to Jesus and remind myself that God loves me and has my life in his hands. But there will likely be days when I lose my grip. *Please, God, keep your steady hand under me, because I'm likely to be shaky some days, and some days I may not even have the energy to crawl. So please be ready to carry me then.* Then again, I know I don't even have to ask. He's been carrying me a long time and sometimes I didn't even know it!

There's another way my current adventure reminds me of those months of pregnancy. Back then, I remember hearing horror stories about pregnancy and especially the delivery process. Being an RN, I had already seen enough deliveries to know it was no picnic, but the dramatic stories of others did not help calm my nerves. It seems nearly everyone who had a baby had a misadventure to tell, and if they lacked a story of their own, they recounted someone else's tale. Usually, these stories did not comfort or encourage, but raised my anxiety instead.

The same thing happens now. Most women who are cancer survivors come forward to offer words of encouragement and hope. They have been great blessings in my life. They offer details only when I ask, and only answer exactly what I asked, offering no embellishment or extra bits of information I'm not ready for. Sometimes I suspect they purposely hold back until I ask questions as they assess my need to know or readiness to hear. But then there are the other well-meaning folks who tell stories of their friends' experiences and sometimes those stories are not good. Their friends are not doing well, the cancer is growing, the cancer has returned, the woman fought hard, but she died. They raise my anxiety and remind me that my killer may be lurking in my body. I long to have a bumper sticker pasted on my chest: "Do not tell me bad cancer stories!" But I won't do that. I've already got way too many issues about my chest.

A couple of women have said to me, "I dealt with the mastectomy just fine. But then, I never was all about my breast." I don't think I'm **all** about my breasts, either, but I'm **some** about them; I do like having them around. I will miss them. Same as if I'd lost a limb, or colon, or some other body part that altered form or function. Same way my dad no doubt misses his legs which still hang on his body but refuse to carry him about as they did before the paralyzing accident. Thankfully, I have an amazing role model in my father. He refused to be bitter or angry or helpless. Even in the hospital, during recovery and rehab, he earned the nickname "Mighty Medlock" because he was determined not to let paralysis define his life or abilities. My dad is the most able man I know. He is also God's man for whatever God wants to do with his life. I'm blessed that he's my dad. The apostle Paul said, "Watch me and do what I do, as I follow Christ."[15] I'm watching you, Daddy, and praying I'll be a worthy disciple, like you. Besides, my boys are watching me.

January 25, Monday

Mary's Song

A few years ago, I was captured by the lyrics of a Christmas song by Amy Grant[16], a meditation on how Mary might have

---

15   *1 Corinthians 11:1*

16   *Amy Grant and Chris Eaton: "Mary's Song."*

felt as she carried the Christ Child in her body. The song speaks to the overwhelming feelings the pregnant young Mary may have experienced and her pleas for God to be with her and enable her on this life journey. That song has been singing to my heart these last several days. If I skip over the first few lines which specifically refer to the Christ Child, most of this song has been the prayer my soul sings to my Savior as I walk this cancer journey. Mary carried the blessing of Jesus in her body. My passenger is quite different, but our needs are similar: Mary needed God to enable her to complete the enormous task to which she was called, and I also need his power and touch on this overwhelming road.

Repeatedly my heart whispers the chorus as I plead with the Lord to keep me together on this journey. The words in the song speak to the parts of me that feel overwhelmed and helpless to control this invader which has attacked my body. They speak to the vulnerability I feel because I am not in control of this disease, and neither are the doctors. Only God can control this one. It will be cured if he orders cure, and it will usher me into eternity if that is his plan. *If it's all the same to you, Lord, I'd like a little longer here on earth with my sons, my husband, and my extended family. I know eternity is wonderful, but I will miss them so.*

Part of me wants to pray: *Lord, you could have stopped it. You didn't.* I have not yet been inclined to ask God why he didn't stop the cancer before it even started. It seems arrogant of me to question his judgment. In his sovereignty, he has permitted this challenge to come into my life and I'm OK with that. Not happy, but resigned to this part of my spiritual and physical journey. I am determined not to spend a great deal of time grieving those things I cannot change.

I've had two bouts with cancer in less than a year's time. I do not believe that God ever wastes any experience and so I believe he has a purpose–or many–for me to walk this path. And that's okay, too. I am confident that God will reveal to me the things I need to understand, will show me those things I'm supposed to do, and hone off the rough edges of my character as he molds me in the image of my Jesus. *Therefore, Lord God, right now, I need your holiness poured over me. I need you to help me be strong, and help me to be the woman you call me to be. Like the lyrics of the song, I need you to simply help me. But mostly, Lord God, hold me together on this journey.*

Mary didn't really know the details of the journey you placed her on when you chose her to carry Jesus. I suspect she didn't anticipate the crucifixion. I certainly didn't anticipate breast cancer. Nevertheless, you have brought me this far in my life and I am confident you will walk the rest of this road with me as well. Just please listen to my heart when I sing these words to you–and hold me together.

Purpose

I have to laugh at myself as I read over the previous words about things being "okay." Like God needed my okay to proceed! He doesn't. I think I'm giving my consent as a way to say, "*I'm willing, Lord, to walk this path for your glory, for my spiritual good, as a witness to your unfailing love even in the midst of a difficult life experience–or whatever else is you purpose here. I am confident as I look down the road of my future that I will be able to praise you for what you will have done in my life and in the lives of those I love. And, Lord, I would be so bold as to ask you to let me be your servant, your ambassador even to people I will never meet on this planet. Let my experience be a spiritual blessing and encouragement to others walking this hard road.*"

This is truly the cry of my heart, that God will use this experience for his glory. I pray that good will come out of it. I'm sure this is the refiner's fire I walk through. I am sometimes perceived as a tough cookie–at least, I think that's my niece's opinion–and I am somewhat direct at times, maybe too direct. At the same time, I'm a rather private person. I suspect that God is knocking off some rough edges, and for sure he's chipping away some of the protective coating I erect around my life at times. He's teaching me to be more of a woman of mercy and grace and less of a woman who wants to take charge and fix things–and people.

I don't think I've prayed for patience (I'm not a fool!) but I suspect that God is building it into my life. I'm a "can do" kind of gal, but for the next several weeks, I'll be sitting on the sidelines while others do even the simplest tasks for me. Initially, I won't be able to fix my hair or dress myself, or maybe even put on makeup. God has certainly forced me into a vulnerable position. I can do nothing but wait for results, wait for people to wait on me, wait for treatment to work, and wait to see if the cancer comes back. And way more of me is out there, exposed, than I'd like it to be. *You've got me in a fine pickle this time, Lord! I hope I don't turn out dill–then again, with all this surgical intervention, I suspect I'll be more like relish–chop, chop. At least make it sweet relish, Lord.*

I'm Not a Singer, But…

The first song that became my accompaniment on this journey was *Mary's Song*, and it continues to be the cry of my heart. A few days ago, another one joined the chorus which sings in my head much of the day: *"We Shall Behold Him"* by Sandi Patti. It is a song about what it will be like to see Jesus face to face when he calls all believers to himself. I think it popped into my head as I was musing about how convenient for me it would be if the Rapture would occur in the next few days. I wouldn't have to waltz through this dance with cancer.

Then, I imagined how it would feel if Jesus snatched me up to meet him in the air after my reconstructive surgery. I would know it was real because the silicone prostheses would suddenly fall out of my chest, replaced by real, beautiful breasts, which only God can make. The scars would be gone and I would be whole again. I would touch my body, suddenly clothed in the righteous robes Christ has promised all of his followers. They will be brilliant white, as he told us, but I embellish the image imagining a soft organza with a flowing wispy quality to the garments. I suppose the robes of the men in the company will be of a more substantial cloth appropriate to the masculine gender.

And then I stopped myself. God will rescue his own, in his own way and time, from whatever trials we face in life. But his Rapture of saints comes only once, and not at my convenience. Besides, there are people I am praying for and they don't yet know my Savior. God will not call for the Rapture until all his chosen ones are gathered in. I stopped my little mind game, but the song has stayed. I imagine what it would be like to see my Jesus, coming in the power described in the Revelation. Some Christians will be walking the earth when that happens. Most of us will already be in heaven with him. I believe we will be that cloud of hosts who accompany him when he comes to reclaim Earth for himself at the end of time as we know it.

I love anticipating the fulfillment of prophecy. Yet for this moment, I have my hands full preparing to face this next private adventure. I won't be raptured out of it, but he will surely be beside me. In the meantime, I enjoy the confidence that I shall behold him, along with all my fellow saints, when the trumpet will sound and the sky will unfold. I know that the rapture will come. Whether I am on this side of eternity or the other, I will see Jesus face to face.

With all these songs rattling around in my head, I suppose I owe Shawn, our church's Worship Minister, an apology. Ward

and I attended his Psalms class on Wednesday nights last fall.
One evening he said, "Music informs our theology." I disagreed.
I believe that our theology informs our music choices.
Furthermore, the truth of God's word in hymns and other
Christian songs speak to our hearts because of the scriptural
truths recorded in the music. Maybe that's what Shawn meant
when he said that, but it sounded to me like he was saying
that music is what we use to form our theological thought. No
doubt Shawn is just way too smart for me in that department,
and several others, too. One thing's for certain, that man sure
can play the piano and about a dozen other instruments to
accompany his singing and to lead our worship times. Probably
when Shawn talks about music and theology, I should just shut
up and learn!

January 27, Wednesday

This Cup

Some of my friends have said, "You are amazing in the way
you are handling this situation"–or something like that. And a
few times, I have responded, "Well, you play the cards you are
dealt." As often as I can, I give God credit for his amazing grace,
which holds me steady in this storm. But I've been mediating
on that response, and it is not quite accurate. I'm not playing
cards from a deck randomly dealt, luck of the draw. I am
drinking the cup my Father has prepared for me. I remember
that Jesus prayed in the Garden of Gethsemane just before the
crucifixion. He asked God to take that cup of suffering from
him, but more importantly, Jesus prayed, "Not my will, but
Thine be done."

I don't believe God willed me to have cancer, but this disease
could not touch me without my Father's permission. This

season is my portion and my cup and I will drink it. Frankly, I don't have much choice in this. God, my Father, has allowed this cup to come into my life. I am a daughter of the Great King. As I take this cup, I get to choose the attitude with which I drink. I can be angry, bitter, resentful, questioning, disappointed, sad, or any of a variety of other emotions. Some of these emotions I have experienced, some may be waiting around some unexpected corner yet unseen.

But I am a daughter of the Great King; therefore, I chose to drink expectantly, trusting that God will use this cup for his glory and for spiritual growth in my life. Furthermore, I believe that he will use my experience to bless others as well. God's economy is always quite efficient. He gets many uses out of each experience in our lives. He teaches lessons whether our response is to turn toward him or away. Don't believe me? Read the Bible. It is full of life lessons from the lives of those who were faithful to God as well as those who rebelled against him, and every behavior in between. God will use this experience as a life lesson, perhaps in many lives. My prayer is that I reflect the sweet image of Jesus, who also drank the cup the Father placed before him. His cup was a much more challenging drink than mine!

This is not the first time I have been aware that God's cups are not always filled with the nectar we would have chosen for ourselves; yet he is able to make even the bitterest drink a blessing in the process and in the ultimate outcome. In January or February of 1992, I was studying the Psalms in my CBS class. Verse 5 of Psalm 16 reads, "Lord, you have assigned me my portion and my cup…" [17] At that time, I was grieving the death of my sister who had been killed instantly in an auto accident a week before Christmas. My response to this great loss was, *"Well, Lord, this is the portion and the cup you have given me and I will drink it."* That verse has stayed with me all these years.

---

17   Psalm 16:5

Although the psalmist probably did not mean it in the way I have applied it to my own life, in a strange way, it is a blessing and comfort. The blessing is what God is doing and will continue to do through this process. The comfort is that he will walk with me through it and also surround me with all that I need for health and life in his kingdom, on Earth or in heaven. Surely, God's "boundary lines have fallen for me in pleasant places; surely I have a delightful inheritance."[18] That's because my boundary lines and ultimate inheritance are not measured in earthly days or years or mileposts. In Christ, I am a free woman, regardless of the places this disease may take me. Ultimately, I walk with my Savior throughout eternity–that's a rich inheritance, which this world, with all its disease and destruction, can never take away from me or anyone who has trusted God. Furthermore, my God has blessed me with many blessings on this earth. My life and days are filled with love from God and family and friends. My moments are drenched in the prayers of the saints who hold me close in this trial. Boundaries?! There are no boundaries with God.

So, Father, thank you for this cup. Fill me with your spirit as I walk through this valley of uncertainty. For surely, there is no uncertainty with you. There is no boundary which can hold me back from experiencing your presence and your love. You will direct my path in pleasant places, regardless of what that path might look like momentarily. You will usher me into your very presence at exactly the moment you have selected–not too soon and not too late. Therefore this cancer, this cup, will accomplish your perfect plan in my life. "I will fear no evil, for thou art with me."[19] Amen and amen.

Cleaning Machine!

I've become a cleaning machine and I'm sure Ward would be thrilled if he realized it. I suspect that he is so preoccupied

---

18   *Psalm 16:6*

19   *Psalm 23*

with what lies before us that he doesn't know how much I clean each day. I see dirt in every corner, on every window and every surface. Even the spaces I cleaned two days ago seem to have collected more dust already and I am driven to remove it. Once I attack one surface, another screams my name, "Clean me! Clean me!" And I oblige.

My weight loss class leader would be proud of me! She constantly encourages us to move more and since I hate to exercise, cleaning seems a productive way to burn calories, release some nervous energy, and deal with those moments of anxious stress. Cleaning like a person possessed beats eating like one, which has been my usual way of shoving emotions off to some other place–which unfortunately usually ends up on my hips or other unsightly spot! So for the moment, I push a vacuum cleaner or wash a window or run another cleaning cloth across some offending surface. Calories burned, house cleaned, stress released.

I suppose part of this drive is knowing that for the next several weeks, I won't be able to reach anything above shoulder height, or lift anything over 10 pounds, or vacuum or scrub for ages. Not that this has bothered me in the past. In fact, I am not known for attention to housekeeping details; there are always so many more interesting things to do, like crafts, reading, writing lectures, socializing on the phone or in person–and shopping! Ward says shopping is my spiritual gift. But I have an urgency to have the house as clean as possible before Tuesday so that when the dust bunnies congregate during my weeks of recovery, at least they will not be joining any senior members of the dirty house society from before February 2. I have made sure of that!

Patience

Well, this is starting to look like a recurring theme, Lord. I was really not eager for a lesson in patience–was that also in the cup

I drank? It's 11:00 AM. I called my cardiologist's office yesterday after 3:00 PM when I realized I need a clearance for surgery .... (Pause to answer phone). Oh, excuse me, Lord. That was Dana from the cardiology office. My appointments are now set up. Thank you. Now, Lord, will you please expedite this clearance so my surgery can go forward if that is your best plan for me? If I'm not supposed to have surgery, please make it really clear. I'm feeling a little anxious, Lord, and if you could make that real clear by tomorrow that would be great. I really need a dose of peace and confidence now. Thank you.

Wow! And Wow!

It's less than a week before surgery and I now have appointments set up with the cardiologist, and some tests, but we will be running down to the last minute to clear me for surgery on February 2. They have archived my records from two and a half years ago, so they will probably have to run a bunch of tests before Tuesday. It occurred to me that my primary care physician would have my records from 2007 when I went through this for another pre-op event. So I called to talk with her triage nurse who has a lovely accent from some other culture, but I couldn't pinpoint it. I told my story, but she said the doctor would not be able to clear me based upon those old records, so I will need to keep moving with the cardiologist. Then, as we were signing off, she said, "Do you believe in God? I thought I heard you say something about God..." I had not said a word about God up to that point, but I responded: "I do believe in God, and I have been praying fervently as have my friends." "Well, I will pray for you, too," she said, and she offered some words of encouragement. Amazed, I thanked her. I know I didn't mention God before she did, but I believe that the Holy Spirit in me spoke to his Spirit in her, no words initially exchanged. God keeps placing his ambassadors in my pathway and I am grateful.

January 29, Friday

A Scheduling Scare

I have been a bit frustrated with the level and timeliness of pre-op information I have received. By last Tuesday, a week before surgery, I still did not know what time the surgery would start or where to report. Fortunately, when I saw my plastic surgeon that afternoon, and began questioning her about surgery schedules and such, she told me she was scheduled to begin reconstruction at 11:00 AM. I went home and called the surgery office to get more details.

I learned that I was to report to the hospital at 7:00 AM on Tuesday, February 2, for pre-op evaluation, with surgery to begin at 9:00 AM. No other pre-op was required because I was not diabetic or hypertensive and there were no other issues on the health form I had filled out when I consulted with them on January 13. And that's when my red flags and anxiety level soared through the roof. I had completed that form within days of receiving my breast cancer diagnosis and was probably still in a little shock. I marked "no heart problems" on the routine check list sheet that was passed to me before I initially met the surgeon, and that is true. I have no heart disease and no cardiac problems. What I do have is a crazy EKG.

I am in great health, but I have a weird EKG pattern–an errant little blip somewhere on that graph. As the first cardiologist who had evaluated and tested me extensively some 18 years ago said, "You have an abnormal EKG in an abnormal way, and there is absolutely nothing wrong." I was again subjected to multiple heart tests 2 ½ years ago when I needed clearance for an outpatient surgical procedure under general anesthesia, and once again the finding was no heart issues, weird EKG. I feared that should they hook me up to a heart monitor on Tuesday, they would cancel my surgery. This cancer has already been in my body way too long–I don't want to wait even one more day. Furthermore, I'm concerned about my reconstructive surgeon's schedule. She is in incredibly high demand in this area and she is the person with whom I will spend most of my surgical experiences in the next year. She rescheduled elective surgeries to take care of me and I don't want her negatively impacted.

The scheduler in the general surgeon's office said I would have to get cardiac clearance and that's when I began my anxious scramble to get appointments, possible tests, and whatever other things were required for surgical clearance. Dana, in the cardiologist's office, is my heroine in this tale. She worked me into the doctor's schedule on Thursday, scheduled tests to hold spots for me should he order such testing, and then I began deep breathing for the next 24 hours. And praying. And questioning. *God, have I missed your plan? Am I not supposed to have surgery? Am I not supposed to have this particular surgery? What if this gets cancelled? Am I supposed to go for a different treatment option?*

I keep hearing my neighbor's voice as she hung over the back fence a few years ago when she told me her doctor found a small cancer in her breast. "I'm having chemo first, before surgery," she said. "They've discovered that's the best way to get all the cancer–shrink the tumor and then remove it." That was not an option offered to me, although I know of some women who have been treated that way. I am telling myself to remember that conversation when I am on the other side of this adventure. I must be careful to emphasize to other women facing this challenge that there are many schools of thought on cancer treatment, many different options, and many effective protocols in place. There is no one right way to treat cancer. In an evolving field, physicians offer the best options they have for the moment. Those options change with each new research study completed.

Medical care and treatment protocols constantly change. I remember several years ago when another friend battled cancer. At one point, her oncologist, a highly respected practitioner in the field, urged a certain treatment regime for her. She prayed and felt strongly led to say no to one particular drug therapy he offered. Two years later, that same oncologist told her if she had chosen the treatment he wanted to administer back then, she would probably be dead. She eventually succumbed to cancer, but she lived longer than she would have had she proceeded with the treatment her doctor first suggested. Her experience reminded me to seek God's wisdom in evaluating the various options offered for my treatment. God is still the Great Physician in all of them.

Intellectually, I know this. Yet in those 24 hours before I saw the cardiologist, I was a wreck. I wish I could say I was calm, and trusting God, and peaceful. But that would be a lie. I was anxious, worried, and feeling totally out of control because of my perception of someone else's ineptitude. There's a saying in the medical community that doctors and nurses make the worst patients, and perhaps that is true. Top that off with my years of training and experience administering a large outpatient department of a major medical center, and I'm sure I have high expectations.

I was also frustrated, and scared, because there was so little time to address the scheduling crunch. One of the testing slots Dana held for me was at 4:00 PM on Monday, February 1–a scant 12 hours before I was due at the medical center where my surgery would occur. This event raised my anxiety level exponentially, I'm sure.

I've already struggled with the various surgical options set before me and I have more peace about surgery first and chemo after if it is necessary. I worry that there is going to be cancer in some nodes, especially because the MRI showed an abnormal node. And I'm ready for chemo, if that's the path before me. In some ways, I almost want it, because I will feel like if there are any errant seed cells floating around in other parts of my body, chemo will wipe them out. *Bottom line, Lord, please direct my surgery and the lab and post-op decisions.*

Long, rambling story short, yesterday my cardiologist cleared me for surgery with no additional testing required. "I think it would be an unnecessary expense to order these tests," he said. I readily concur. My anxiety flew out the window, my peace about surgery returned, and I reminded myself about what my friend, Connie, also a nurse, said last Sunday, "Don't second guess yourself." I'm trying not to, Connie, I'm trying not to. But it is hard being an RN, as you well know!

I called Ward and met him for lunch. Then I came home, feeling free as a bird, and took the dog for a walk in the beautiful afternoon sun–60 degrees on a January day in Virginia! God's little present to me before the great confinement. Of course, the great confinement actually starts tomorrow: Richmond is expected to get 6–10 inches of snow!

Friday's Ramblings

Now it is Friday, 9:50 AM and the surgeon's office has just called to say they realized they forgot to tell me to be at the hospital at 7:00 AM for an 8:00 AM procedure regarding the lymph nodes. The scheduler apologized that she had overlooked telling me about the node procedure. I appreciated her candor. I am so glad she took the time to call and tell me about this additional procedure so I wouldn't be anxious or confused on the morning of my surgery.

Since this mastectomy, I've learned that pre-op clearances and tests are handled much differently than when I was trained as a nurse many years ago. Today, pre-op clearances are actually determined by the anesthesiologists who are responsible for keeping patients both sedated and alive through surgery. There are different protocols in different facilities, and in many cases, no pre-op clearance is required beyond the patient's health report. Because my weird EKG means nothing, I forget about it until I'm in a situation like this one where it could have a negative impact on the timing of surgery. I won't forget this minor detail in the future, and I now carry a copy of my cardiologist's report with me when I go to a new physician!

Alyse called and talked for a long time, letting me ask lots of questions about what to expect immediately after surgery and during the recovery process. She answered questions about how I might feel, what I would be able to do, lots of those practical kinds of questions about how my body would function and what limitations I would likely experience. I am so grateful to Alyse. She helps me anticipate my needs and recovery. She also is a source of encouragement as she shares ways to cope with the upcoming process. She is a Godsend!

She also said, in response to my many concerns about pain management, "Carolyn, I don't think the pain or the disability is going to be nearly as bad or as limiting as you are expecting." I hope she is right and I am wrong. It is true that I am anticipating this surgery through the lens of my experiences as a nursing student in the late 70s when I had my breast augmentation. Back then, it was a brutal procedure and I could barely breathe, except shallow breathes, for days, much less lift my arms. But medicine has come a long way since the 1970s.

My precious CBS Powhatan ladies came to visit this afternoon. Gwen, Judy and Carol came bearing food, flowers, and priceless cards and notes written by the leadership and members of the Powhatan class. They stayed to visit and laugh and offer encouragement. It was great to laugh! After they left, I opened and read each of the cards. What a powerful experience! Each card carried words of encouragement, scripture, prayer, and blessing. As I read the cards and names of the writers, I smiled, envisioning each woman as she penned those words–words of life, and hope, and promise; words of comfort and healing and blessing. Jesus wrapped himself in the skins of these precious Powhatan women and smiled at me today.

Thank you, Lord, for the sweet kiss of your word; thank you for your fresh love poured upon me in the words of your daughters across the river. I am so blessed to be part of your great big family! While my mother and my blood sister reside in your house, you have not left me alone, but have surrounded me with a huge family of sisters and brothers in Christ. Thank you that you have expanded my tents to include such a family of life and hope and promise.

Chapter 2: FEBRUARY
Surgery and More

February 1, Monday

The Day Before …

It's another Monday. This is the last day before surgery and I would be lying to say I am not nervous. I have many things to accomplish today to be ready for the morning and I planned it that way so I am not sitting here all day just thinking about tomorrow. I believe I will come through surgery fine, minus the girls, and with their temporary stand-ins in place. Having said that, I know that sometimes people die unexpectedly in some surgical mishap. Or the cancer could be spread everywhere. I currently over-interpret every signal my body sends and worry that it has metastasized. It is probably the normal reaction of every cancer patient and I am no different, with one exception. I believe I am held in the tender hands of my Savior and I know that if I die, I will be with him in paradise. I am also confident that I will see my loved ones again.

Having said that, I must write these words in the unlikely event that I have already seen my boys for the last time on this earth: I LOVE YOU BOTH with ALL MY HEART. I typed those words in shouts of love, which I want you to hear through the years–I'll be waiting for you in heaven, don't disappoint me. Dig deeply into God's word, and strive to build a strong relationship with him through Jesus. Andrew, I know that you grapple right now with good questions about some of the hard issues in scripture. Pray, seek God's direction and guidance, and he will give you the answers in his words, and in his Word. You have a strong spiritual foundation and a heart of gold. Keep a teachable spirit.

David, keep on growing spiritually. Pray and seek God's direction for your life's work and he will show you where to serve him; perhaps in a career you do not even know exists at this moment. I didn't find my real career place until I moved into hospital administration. I didn't know an MPA degree existed until about six weeks before I was enrolled in that graduate program! And my real life's call wasn't in a job at all. It was in raising you and Andrew and serving God in a variety of places, CBS being the most major place. Just walk with him, and he will show you where to go. Same for you, Andrew. In all your life decisions, boys, seek God's direction. Sometimes he only shows us the pathway one step at a time. But keep walking and all will be revealed.

Ward, you are the love of my life and more than I could have ever dreamed or hoped for in a husband. I am so sorry to leave you this soon–I meant to grow old with you. I envisioned our 50th wedding anniversary as we walked strong, hand in hand, into the place where we would celebrate with family and friends. I would be 85, but smiling and erect in posture, slim, (I can dream, can't I?) with the beauty of Christ as my major adornment. You would be handsome as always, my prince, my champion. We would be surrounded by beautiful grandchildren. If you are reading this in the next few weeks, I will already be in heaven. But I will wait for you there. In the meantime, please marry again if you meet someone with whom you will be happy, and enjoy the blessings of another woman who will love you dearly. There is no marriage in heaven, so we will all be brothers and sisters in Christ, and I will be glad to see you both.

Andrew, David, Ward–I love you, I love you, I love you!

Tracy and Michael Wayne, I also love you both dearly. My prayer is that you will make Christ the center of your lives. Put aside all that has gone before in your lives, bloom in the places God has planted you. Put aside all bitterness, reject the lies of the devil who would try to lead you astray and convince you that all is hopeless. That's a lie. Claim and live Jeremiah 29:11. Live the hope. I will see you in eternity.

Daddy, you are a wonderful man. You have pointed so many people to Christ. You modeled his love in the tender way you cared for Mother, and I remember that you stuck with her through some very hard times. You sacrificed a lot of yourself and your dreams for your marriage and family. Thank you for blazing a trail for me to show me how to face adversity and come out stronger in spirit and in faith in Jesus Christ our Lord. I'll see you there! I love you.

February 23, Tuesday

Catching Up the Story

Since I last wrote in this journal, a lot has transpired. My surgery was on February 2, and went well. The love letter to my family did not have to be delivered, because, as I had hoped and expected to, I survived! I spent two nights in the hospital. Ward spent the first night with me, on a tiny recliner which was more for looks than comfort, and Pat Rudd came the first afternoon after surgery and spent that second night with me.

Mostly I was able to convince people to refrain from visiting. I have a theory that if you are sick enough to be hospitalized post op, then you are too sick for visitors. My pastor wanted to come the morning of surgery and pray with me and Ward pre-op, but I begged him not to come. I felt bad about that, but I just couldn't get my head around my pastor praying with me about having my boobs cut off. I knew God would hear his prayers very clearly from his office, and I would be spared the embarrassment of being seen ugly and draped in a shapeless gown with no make-up. (I never said I wasn't vain!)

My dad and his wife did come the day after surgery, after I had begged them not to come on the day of surgery. I do not do well with free-floating anxiety around me, and especially pre-surgery. Following surgery I don't want to see anyone and I don't want to be seen, either. Surgery is nasty business and I prefer to do it pretty much alone, except for the one person who will be my advocate and protector. The first night, that person was Ward, and Pat took the second night.

I do remember that Michael Wayne popped in for a few minutes that first night to check on me. It was a pleasant surprise, but sad to say I rewarded his efforts by throwing up the lame liquids they had given me for dinner! He didn't stay long. They had me up going to the bathroom the day of surgery and by the next morning I was out walking the halls. I do remember one funny walk, probably day two in the evening, when Dick dropped by, Ward was still there, and Pat had arrived for her tour of duty. All four of us went walking down the hall, someone pushing my IV pump, and I felt like a regal, if shabby-looking, queen with her entourage. I think they pulled my morphine pump that night.

I'm a good patient, but I have a shy bladder. I don't pee on command very well, and I certainly don't pee for an audience. They had pulled my catheter in the recovery room, which I thought was a stupid thing to do. So, here I am in pain, in compression boots, with IV pumps, and I have to keep getting up to try to go to the bathroom when I didn't really feel like it. The evening nurse kept coming in and saying, "If you don't pee, we'll have to bring the sonogram in to see what's wrong." And my feeling was, "Is that supposed to be some kind of threat to make me pee? I don't have anything to pee. I'm throwing it up out of my mouth!" But eventually the bladder does what it's supposed to do–I peed. And my waterworks continued to function properly for the next 24 hours.

Then, the second night a new nurse came on the late shift. Now if you've ever been in the hospital, you know that they wake you up several times a night to take vitals and ask you stupid questions like "Are you sleeping okay?" This new nurse had a different question, though. She woke me up to say "Are you peeing?"

"NO!" I said, probably too rudely. "I don't pee at night! I sleep at night! I pee in the day!"

I'm not sure she'd gotten that answer before and it came back to haunt her a couple of weeks later.

Happily, I went home the next day where no one awoke me in the middle of the night to ask dumb questions. In no time at all, I was up and about, doing nearly anything I wanted to do. The pain level was much less severe than I had expected, and recovery was swift. My biggest challenge was to remember not to do too much physically because I felt great! Pat did come back to my house the afternoon I was discharged and spent that afternoon and early evening with me. We planned to wash my hair the following day when she returned. Mother Nature nearly sidetracked that plan. It began snowing early in the morning and started piling up fast. Pat's husband had business to attend to a couple of counties away, so he dropped Pat at my house and I got my first shampoo in days. It felt glorious!

We had a record-breaking winter of snow here in the west end of Richmond in the winter of 2009-10. Several big snows totaled more than 47 inches at my home. It was easy to be confined to home recovering from surgery, because snow confined everyone else to their homes as well. I think that was God's little blessing for me! I didn't miss anything much that everyone else wasn't also missing for weather reasons. I was happy and looking forward to moving on to recovery.

And then it happened. On Monday, February 15, in the late afternoon I noticed that my right chest area, around the incision, was red and hot to touch. I called my plastic surgeon immediately who told me to start taking antibiotics and come into her office the next morning, which I was already scheduled to do for an expansion. She did not do the expansion but increased the antibiotics and scheduled me back for Wednesday morning. Wednesday morning I arrived expecting a quick check by her and return to home. Instead she ordered me straight to the hospital; didn't even want me to go home for clothes. I assured her I could be quick, especially since most of my stuff from my surgical admission was still in a suitcase in my bedroom.

I ended up on the fourth floor of the same hospital again, this time across the hall from my previous room. My dear friend Jan arrived about the time I got assigned a room and I was so happy to see her. In contrast to the previous admission for surgery, when I knew I would look and feel terrible, this time I actually felt great and looked pretty good, too! I was eager for company, and as the days stretched on, friends were a welcome distraction from the monotony of days punctuated by the changing of the IV bags and the serving of the meals.

The Medical Center, where I was once again housed, is a new facility and if one has to be hospitalized, it's a great place to be. All the rooms are private, with silk curtains and elegant furniture. It's like a classy hotel. To top it all, patients phone in their meal orders selected from a fine restaurant style menu. There are lots of choices, just call dining, place your order, and give them the time you'd like your meal delivered. Furthermore, one guest meal can also be ordered for a nominal fee. Ward and I began to have dinner-date nights in my room. The food was good, not five star, but good for institutional food. My admission stretched to five days, I felt great but was tied to an IV pump most of the day and night, so I amused myself with ordering from the nice menu. I think I gained a pound a day. Thank goodness I was finally discharged or I might have had to be taken out on a forklift.

The nurses loved me because I felt great, could take care of most of my needs without help and placed little demands upon their time. Some of them learned that I'm a nurse, and they actually would stop by and just chat now and then, a pleasant break for them, I suppose, and a very welcome treat for me. And then one day, in walks a nurse who says, "Don't I know you? Weren't you here recently?"

"Yes," I said, "I'm the double mastectomy who was across the hall a couple of weeks ago." And then I remembered and added, "I'm the one you woke up in the middle of the night to ask me if I peed, and I told you I pee in the day and sleep in the night."

We both laughed, but I noticed the next night that she was not assigned to me. I don't know if that was coincidence, but I do know she didn't wake me up to ask if I was peeing.

I did have a couple of other interesting night experiences though. One night, one of the aides awoke me about 3 AM to take my vitals. The nurse was hooking up more IV meds at that point, so I suppose the aide decided to entertain me. He went off on some long story, I think about his son or something, and I'm lying there thinking, "Please be quiet, I just want to sleep; I'm not feeling very social." I guess it must get lonely in the middle of the night but there must have been some poor soul who couldn't sleep and would have loved company. I wasn't one of those. The following night, I was please to awaken in the morning and discover that I had slept all night. The nurses had come in and made the IV changes, but I slept through that, too. "How'd I manage to sleep through vitals last night?" I asked my early morning nurse.

"Oh, we were short on nursing assistants last night so they didn't get taken."

"That was great for me," I replied. And after that I prayed for a nursing assistant shortage every night.

My admission had initially been planned for three days, but I had bad veins and that delayed treatment for a day while we waited for a PICC line to be placed. Then I had a drug reaction which created another treatment delay and then the infection spread. Finally, the sixth day after my admission, I was sent home on home health IV therapy. I hated every minute of it. It really wasn't that bad, but I despised the PICC line hanging out of my arm and I hated taking care of my lines–flushing, heparin locks, all the infection control issues. I hated nursing when I was in practice and I certainly didn't want to be my own nurse.

To add insult to injury, the infection control doctor, who was supposed to remove my line after 10 days, decided that I needed another week of IV therapy. I did not have a good attitude about that! I think she over-reacted to redness in my chest area caused by the tight bra with padding which I wore in to her office. I had not looked red when I left the house that morning. But her little office assistant, who had somehow been promoted to … I don't know what … also set me off when she placed me in the room. She flipped open my chart and said, "Well, I see your white count is fine, but your CRP is a little high and so is your SED rate."

"I know what a SED[1] rate is," I said. "What is CRP?" I didn't remember that test from my nursing practice years.

"That's a marker of infection" she responded authoritatively.

"Yes, but what does CRP stand for?" I asked.

"It's just a marker of infection."

"But what do the letters mean?" I pressed for an explanation.

"I don't know, it just tells us there's still infection present," she answered.

---

1   *SED is a short-hand medical term for the blood test called Erythrocyte Sedimentation Rate. It is one indicator of inflammation in the body.*

I was not impressed that an office girl seemed to be interpreting my lab results for me, using terms she appeared reluctant or unable to explain. I was not a happy camper. When I asked the doctor what CRP stood for, she gave me the same answer: "An infection marker." I was frustrated that I couldn't get a simple answer for what those letters represented.

I went home and searched the internet. It turns out CRP stands for C-reactive protein. Now that wasn't so hard. Why didn't they just tell me that to start with? But a little more research confirmed my suspicions. It's a very weak marker and was only identified a few years ago. It can be falsely high in obese patients (unfortunately I fit that medical category, although I don't think I'm that big!), and in patients with cancer. Hello … I just had surgery for cancer–did anybody read my chart? Besides that, it is currently used as a predictor of heart disease or likelihood of stroke, and is higher in people with a variety of autoimmune diseases including arthritis, rheumatism, and several other isms. I don't know of any "isms" I have, but then again, I'm sixty! There could be unidentified isms all over the place! At any rate, I thought it was a very bad reason to keep me on potent IV drugs another week, especially since my white count was normal,I feared that my ability to get a portacath placed was about to be jeopardized. I was afraid my chemo would not start in a timely manner. I felt like a Roman candle about to explode!

The next morning when I woke up, my chest had returned to normal color again–no red or pink present after a good night's sleep with no binding clothing and falsies to fill out the bra cups. I called the Infectious Disease doctor's office to explain my finding, got the office girl, and pleaded for my PICC line to be pulled early. She contacted the doctor, who refused to pull the line early and refused to listen to my current condition as well. I was frustrated and angry.

At any rate, I telephoned my general surgeon and persuaded his nurse to schedule me for the portacath the day after I was scheduled to see the infectious disease doc the following Wednesday. I assured her the PICC line would be out. Then I asked my home health nurse how to remove a PICC line and told her very clearly that it would be removed either by the doctor or by me, but it would not be in my body past Wednesday. Whether or not she communicated this to the doctor, I do not know. Furthermore, I discontinued my IV drugs the day before my visit to the Infectious Disease doc. I was not willing to play that game anymore. She took the line out the next day. In fact, it was the young office girl who removed it, not applying pressure like the visiting nurse had instructed me to do. When I questioned her, she said it wasn't necessary, so I crossed my arms and subtly applied pressure myself when she turned her back. I still don't know if it was necessary or not, but I did not want a big bruise there, and I did not get one.

In cooler-headed moments, I understand why nurses and doctors are sometimes considered the worst patients, and I'm sure I've worn that label more than once. But it is very frustrating to feel that I'm not being listened to, or worse, to feel that I'm being talked down to. I expect to be heard, and I want to feel that those delivering care to me are familiar with the details of my medical condition and history. I know that I spend plenty of time in every office I enter filling out patient history forms and I hope those are read and taken into account when care is planned for me. But sometimes it feels to me like the paperwork is just being completed as a legal exercise.

I also understand why Americans are frustrated with health care, even though I must say in spite of these few little missteps, I believe I have mostly received medical care comparable to none. I know that my prognosis is as good as it is because my medical care was accomplished with great speed. My surgery was performed 3 ½ weeks after diagnosis, and my rapidly growing tumor came in just under the Stage Two marker. Stage One feels to me like a much better place to be than Stage Two, even if I am only separated from a Stage Two by one tenth of a centimeter. I don't know that such quick treatment would have happened in any other country, and I am exceeding grateful for this positive chance at life–and cure! And I'm finished with my little soap box for today; thank you very much for listening!

2011 Update: On reflection, the rest of February passed blissfully uneventfully for me. I went back to my Bible study class in the Far West End. I was stunned when I walked into the leadership class and was greeted with a standing ovation. I hadn't expected that! I thought I would just walk in like normal, just a gal who had been absent for a few weeks. I hope I reacted graciously without showing the embarrassment I felt. I knew their applause was intended as a warm welcome home and a celebration of all God has been doing. I was surprised and grateful for their warmth and love. I just didn't want to be the center of attention for getting a nasty disease–what a lousy claim to fame!

Chapter 3: MARCH
Round One of Chemo

March Musings

As the month of March rushed toward more surgery to place a portacath for chemotherapy commencement, I rushed around trying to prepare for the inevitable changes these medical procedures would bring. I had more doctor visits, more pre-op testing, and I began to gather the accouterments of the chemo patient: hats and scarves and wigs. I didn't write every day, or even every week, but I jotted down little thoughts here and there as I moved through the moments of the month.

March was not all dread and worry, however. Andrew received his acceptance letter to Dental School early in the month and Ward and I began the search for property to purchase near the medical university he would attend. We reasoned that the money we would spend for housing might as well be paid to us, and we settled on a townhouse in my favorite section of our city. In the house-hunting process, I met a real estate agent named Lacy who has become a great friend and we had some good adventures in the real estate process.

Following are some of my random thoughts and experiences, not necessarily in exact order because as life rushed at me, I grabbed onto snatches of activity and scrapes of paper for hastily written thoughts. And I tried to remember to breathe, even when issues seemed stifling.

March 4, Thursday

All Things Pink

Whether you mean to or not, once you become a breast cancer patient, pink becomes your hot new color. Friends give pink gifts in pink bags often with the symbolic pink breast cancer ribbon on it. Last Sunday after church, Martha handed me a beautiful pink gift bag with a lovely fleece blanket tucked inside. It's a fleece prayer blanket made of the symbolic pink and tied all around with pink ribbons. Each ribbon represents a prayer some sweet woman has offered up to God on my behalf: prayers for healing, full recovery, his comfort and encouragement as I go through chemo.

But my blanket also included three white ribbons, precious prayers from Sherra, a dear sister of the household of faith who now lives in Kentucky. I was privileged to serve with Sherra in CBS after she and her husband left the South American mission field because of her own serious illness. Sweet Sherra, who taught me so much about prayer as she served as Prayer Chairman for our CBS class, is now my prayer warrior as well. Later in the week, I received a card and note of encouragement from Sherra, another treasure I've added to the growing stack of cards and letters, which arrive daily at my house. Nearly all of those notes include prayers, encouraging words, and scriptures that remind me that our awesome God holds each of us in his hand.

I will take this blanket with me when I go to chemo. I'll tuck it into the pink tote bag Nancy brought to me when she gave me the Kim Newlen camisole. I'll proudly drink from the pink BPA-free water bottle which will help me keep track of the many glasses of water I must consume each day to flush out the left-overs from the medicines intended to clean up any errant cancer seed cells.

I'm beginning to understand how teachers must feel when they receive the wide assortment of apple-clad gifts, which we've come to associate with that noble profession. Whether or not she was an apple fan before she became a teacher, I envision a red room somewhere in each teacher's house, which sports these gifts of love and gratitude. I know I'll never look at the color pink in the same way again. Once upon a time, I associated pink with my mother because it was her favorite color. I even decorated in pink the handicap-adapted suite that we built for her on the back of our house after her stroke. I still think of Mother, of course, when I see pink.

But now pink also represents a whole new source of blessing. Each pink item which has come into my house says there's another sweet woman who loves me and wishes me healing and health. Each pink present represents a heart of love and weaves a spirit of prayer around me like a sweet pink bubble. For the rest of my life, when I see pink, I will remember how much I am loved by my earthly family and my spiritual family. I'll see not only the pink breast cancer ribbon, but also the hearts of love poured out for me in so many overwhelming ways. *Thank you, God, that you continue to make your presence known to me in such tangible ways, including pink gifts of practicality. From this day forward, I'll also think of pink as my personal call to praise you, my Savior and my God, for you are worthy of our praise.*

Clear Directions

I have asked God to make my pathway clear as I navigate these cancerous waters, and he has been more than faithful. At each turn, I have gotten his guidance, and more importantly, his peace. For example, I saw an oncologist on Friday to whom I had been referred by my surgeon. He and I didn't have any conversations about oncologists. I simply got a phone call from an office employee informing me that I had been scheduled for an appointment with such and such a doctor. When I questioned the caller about how my doctor had chosen this particular oncologist, she had no clue. Since there are dozens of oncologists in this city, it seemed to me there had to be some process of selection, but I wasn't included in that loop. I was puzzled and frustrated. It seemed to me that a decision of this level of importance should have included some conversation with me.

I have since learned that more and more physicians attach themselves to hospital-based medical groups. As an employee of a medical corporation, they refer within that organization. Those affiliated with other medical entities apparently don't usually get considered for referral. I suppose breast cancer has become so commonplace within the medical community that there is no urgency to look beyond one's corporate borders, but this model did not fit my personality or experience.

The model had worked in my favor when I was first diagnosed. My OB/GYN had already scheduled a surgical appointment for me before I had even received the results of the biopsy. The radiologist gave me the appointment card at the same time he delivered the "C Word" news. I only had to wait five days to see the surgeon and he turned out to be a great match for me. But the truth of the matter is that he would do his best work in the two or three hours that I slept the deep anesthesia sleep, while the oncologist would be my frequent care provider for the short term, and a doctor I'll see for the rest of my life. Actually, I don't know that a surgeon ever discharges a cancer patient, either, but I was pretty sure I'd be seeing my oncologist a lot more frequently. I wanted to be sure of a good personal match with my oncologist.

I kept the oncology appointment, which the surgeon's office set for Friday, February 26. Ward accompanied me to the consultation. I know I was anxious about the visit, filled with questions I didn't even know to ask, just undefined question marks floating round me like a cartoon character. I felt like a prisoner recently condemned to a place I didn't want to be. The visit started off a bit rough when the young office assistant measured me at 5'5". Since I'm really 5' 6 ½" barefoot and claim 5'7", I was shocked with her measurement and questioned her. She looked me up and down and said, "Oh, no, you aren't nearly that tall! You're no more than 5'5" at the most!" I was not happy. What if they mixed drugs like they measured patients–I'd be in a pickle. I stewed a few minutes until the doctor arrived.

She was nice, gracious to answer all my questions patiently. She reviewed a couple of study protocols they were doing. I told her I planned to consult with another oncologist as well for a second opinion. I suppose I was hoping someone would say, "You don't really need chemo", but her answer let me know that would not happen. As she turned me over to an RN for a facility tour, she said, "If you decide not to get chemo here, that's fine. But please call my office and let me know where you are going. I just want to be sure you are getting treatment." At that moment, any tendency toward denial vanished. I was pretty sure the question was not, "Do I need chemo?" but instead, "Where shall I get chemo treatment?"

As the nurse led me into the waiting room, the first person I saw was obviously a chemo patient awaiting her turn at treatment. She wore a turban over her head and her Caucasian skin was some odd color between gray, taupe and tan. I feared I was seeing the near future me. I felt sorry for the woman and sick to my stomach. It was a sad and scary day. The chemo room was a large, open space facing a lovely outdoor garden with beautiful stonework and evergreens. The wall of windows seemed to stretch two or three stories tall and lounge chairs were grouped around TVs so that patients could watch programs or chat with their neighbors while they infused. Some people like this community model, and the view was lovely, but the setting was not appealing to me. It felt cold and cavernous. We left and I did not have a peaceful feeling.

I had decided from the beginning that I would consult at the university cancer center in town. After all, that's a tertiary care facility. Both Ward and I trained there, and while it would not be my first choice for a hangnail, I had always said if I had something really wrong with me, that was the place to go. So, I set up an appointment with one of their oncologist who specialized in breast cancer treatment. I took along my friend, Michelle, who is an RN. I couldn't see any reason for Ward to cancel his own patients to go with me on another consultation. He was already trying to catch up patient appointments from the patients he rescheduled during my original surgery. I didn't want him to have to move more of his patients.

Besides, Michelle is an RN with experience at the Mayo Clinic where she was a research nurse and also a transplant coordinator. Her titles are probably much more impressive than what I've written here, but trust me, her knowledge base and experience is amazing. She probably knows more about nursing in her little finger than all the nursing I knew when I left the field after three years as a head nurse. I wanted her impression of the facility and the treatment plan. I wanted her finely-tuned ears to hear what the doctor said to me.

This oncologist offered me several treatment options. More importantly, she offered her encouragement, her compassion, and her promise that she would find the right treatment to fight this cancer with me. She treated me like I was her only patient and we left the clinic long after the clerical staff had left for the day. She had a bubbly personality, had initially introduced herself with her first name, no "Dr." title before it, and made me feel like I'd just found a long lost friend. More importantly, she was a wealth of knowledge about my kind of cancer and shared survival statistics for my particular age and stage and type of cancer. I left there confident that I had found my home for this phase of the journey. Michelle never imposed her impressions on me until I spoke first. We talked about options on the way home and she helped me sort out my thoughts.

Furthermore, there was a research protocol which was a possibility. After I got home and read it, more thoroughly mentally processing the details, I felt I did not want to be part of that study. I asked God to help me make the right decision and had peace that I would not join that protocol. Today, the oncologist emailed me that I am not a candidate for that particular study because of the melanoma last summer. I take that as confirmation from God who has closed a door that was not intended for me. I'm going to ask my doctor to treat me with a chemo agent that would work well on melanoma too, just in the event that some of those evil little cells also escaped undetected. *Lord God, I may not know it on this earth, but wouldn't it be just like you to give me this particular kind of breast cancer to cause me to get the drugs which would kill those melanoma cells! I'll bet you have lots of surprises waiting for me up there in heaven. We're going to have some great talks, I just know it*!

Treasures of the Heart

I have been overwhelmed with the outpouring of love from so many people in unexpected ways and places. For example, one of the children's teachers at CBS came to me today during leadership and handed me a simple plastic shopping bag saying that she had been thinking about me and wanted to give me something special. Jean had decided on the item inside because it had been her mother's and had comforted her when she was ill.

Jean is a quiet lady, about my age, soft-spoken, not prone to talk much in our large leadership group. She and I bonded early in our CBS ministry and she is a blessing to the children she serves in our children's ministry. I looked in the bag and there was a small stuffed bear with a poem on it about a "burden bear". Attached to the little bear was a scripture verse from I Peter 5:7: "Cast all your cares upon Him for He cares for you," a sweet reminder that God cares about all our concerns and can handle them. Jean explained that this bear had been her mother's when she was sick and now she wanted me to have it as I go through these treatments. "If you want to," Jean said, "you can pass it on to someone else in the future who may be facing a tough situation." I was touched by this tender gift, a treasure from Jean's heart to mine and it reminded me of another precious heart gift I had received from my sister many years before.

When I graduated from nursing school, my sister presented me a gift with a note explaining its importance to her. It was a lovely ring with a yellow tiger-eye stone which her husband Mike had commissioned for her when they lived in Georgia. They had spotted a similar one at a craft show and ordered it on the spot. She said that this ring was a ring she loved. It represented a special time in her life when they were very happy and she wanted me to have it. I still have the note she wrote, and the ring is a treasure I will cherish until I pass it on one day to her daughter, Tracy.

March 12, Friday

Pink Butterfly Luncheon

Today the Butterflies met at Kate's house for lunch. I had been looking forward to this day to gather with my prayer buddies. I knew they would hold me in their hearts as I begin chemo. What I had not anticipated was a luncheon planned to honor me. When we stepped into the dining room, we were greeted with a beautifully set table, decked out all in pink. At each place setting, Kate had carefully placed several items with the pink breast cancer emblem, including a pen, a bracelet, and some embroidered ribbons. At my spot, her husband had also left a denim "hat of hope", a cancer drug promotional item from the pharmaceutical company for which he works. It's a cool looking hat with words of affirmation and hope embroidered all over it. I will celebrate the God of Hope when I wear it over my bald head. Kate showed me the pink ribbon she hung on her refrigerator for me–a call to pray for me when she enters the kitchen. Once again, I find myself enveloped in a loving pink bubble. Oh, how I've come to treasure the color pink and all the love and hope it represents in my life!

March 16, Tuesday

First Chemo Treatment

The week before my first chemotherapy treatment, I met with my oncologist at the satellite infusion center not far from my home where my chemo treatments take place. When I walk in for this first treatment, I'm greeted by the welcoming and familiar face of the nurse who had drawn my pre-treatment lab work the prior week. I feel comfortable at this facility. It is a modern structure with individual cubicle-like rooms encircling a nurse's station, much like an emergency room or an ICU. The nurses can see everyone with an easy sweep of the space, while each patient is afforded a measure of privacy from the other patients. Each cubicle is furnished with a big comfy recliner, a table, a cable television, a work counter for the nurse and a wall of cabinetry. A big window lets in sunlight and permits the patient to relax and look beyond the confines of the IV tether while the chemicals infuse. Or the window coverings can be drawn and the lights turned low for a little nap. I like the closeness of the room. I leave the curtains open but settle in to the little cocoon for my treatment regime. I feel protected and at peace.

While the medication does it work, patients are offered drinks and snacks by a volunteer who periodically passes through the space offering refreshment, a smile and words of encouragement if one wants to talk. There's room in the cubicle for the patient to bring along a couple of friends or family for company, but I have chosen to come alone. I had been instructed not to drive myself home from treatment, so a neighbor on her way to work dropped me off for my first treatment and another friend will pick me up and bring me home. Many friends offered to be my drivers and companions during my treatment, but I prefer to do this alone. I'm armed with my cell phone and my husband's laptop. I have a book and my ever-present Sudoku book. If I want to, I'll nap in the big comfy chair or I'll borrow one of the hundreds of movie CDs which a volunteer offers to retrieve for me from the treatment center's library. I chose to use this morning to read and play my Sudoku puzzles.

The infusion process itself is fairly uneventful for me. But I am surprised by a couple of people I meet this morning. First, there is the Monkey Lady. She walks through carrying a basket of long-armed stuffed monkeys in a rainbow of colors. Their Velcro hands permit them to hang from the IV pole or dangle from a cabinet doorknob or chair arm. She uses them to share a smile and a few words of encouragement if invited. It's a gift of love with a silly stuffed monkey as an icebreaker. She told me she buys them by the caseload and distributes them at the urging of the son of one of her friends. He had battled cancer and was the first recipient of a long-armed hanging monkey. He urged her to turn this one kind deed for him into a ministry to other cancer patients and so that's what she does. She dispenses sunshine, kindness and diversion as she offers little stuffed monkeys to those who are getting chemo. As she turns to leave my cubicle, I smile at my little monkey friend and carefully tuck him into my tote bag for our trip home.

My next surprise visitor was the lady pushing the refreshment cart. I recognized her immediately as the school nurse from my boys' years in middle school. She stopped to chat and I learned that this volunteer opportunity was one of those activities she chose after her sons, like mine, graduated and went on to college and the world of young adulthood. I was further surprised to learn she is married to a surgeon affiliated with this medical complex where I'm getting treatment. I guess it is a small world after all.

The morning passes quickly and I am soon picked up by my friend and delivered safely back to my house. I am surprised to feel no different in the afternoon than I did in the morning. "Is this how I can expect to feel after each treatment?" I asked the nurse who checked me out. She answered in the affirmative. "So I can actually drive myself to treatments? Because I feel fine." Again, affirmative. I was excited to be free to transport myself to and fro for the next treatment cycle. This had been easier than I expected.

March 20, Thursday

After-Effects of First Treatment

Day Two following chemo is going well. I feel good and the challenges of yesterday are gone. Yesterday was a little rough. I woke up lightheaded and that stayed with me all morning, subsiding by early afternoon. I had planned to drive myself back to the infusion center to get the injection designed to boost white cell output quickly after a treatment. Alas, with the dizziness, I was afraid to drive so I scrambled around to find someone to take me. Bless Catherine's heart—she is another longtime friend and nurse. She ditched her husband (she works a few days a week in his dental office) and came to ferry me to my appointment.

I reported my symptoms to the nurse administering the injection, but she said dizziness was not a usual symptom of the medications I am on. However, I've read the literature, and it is one of the less common ones which need to be reported, and I told her that. She said if they continued for 24 hours, call back. By mid-afternoon, they were gone and the dog and I took a walk. She's old and I'm fragile right now, so we are a good match. Part of my treatment is to exercise regularly, so I hope I don't kill her for my cure. She seems to enjoy our little adventures, and it's certainly not a strenuous outing.

Besides the lightheadedness, consuming copious amounts of liquids, and multiple trips to the bathroom (does that count as exercise?), I woke up eight pounds lighter this morning. My doctor says she doesn't want to see more than 20 pounds weight change one way or the other over the next few months of treatment. At this rate, I'll be reaching my limit in 2 ½ treatments. Oh, the injustice of finding an effective weight loss program and being told not to lose weight! Well, at least my plastic surgeon is making sure I get chesty! That's some consolation, even though it feels like two rocks on my chest where breasts used to be. I hope the permanent implants will be a little softer, but then again, there's nothing on top of them but muscle.

Will I Get to Grow Old?

On Sunday Ward and I went to a Wendy's restaurant for a quick supper. In the booth behind us was an ancient man who kept begging the equally elderly woman to make whoopee with him. I heard way more of their conversation than I wanted to because our alarm system people called to say our alarm was going off at our home. We were only blocks from home, so Ward left me at the restaurant for a few minutes to check on the house. I heard the old guy call the lady "Wifey" and talk about how he wished they could get together to make whoopee. He said it was nice that her granddaughter had been willing to bring her up from another state to see him. I wondered if they were separated because of ill health and thought it sad that they weren't in a nursing home together. But who knows, they may have both been so confused that the whole story I heard was wrong. But it made me very sad to think of two old people who had once had a life together and were now separated by miles and circumstances beyond their choice. I wondered: Will Ward and I have old years together? I cried.

Waterlogged

In my efforts to be the best little chemo patient ever, still trying to control an uncontrollable situation, I suppose, I diligently followed the instructions in some of the literature I was given which said to drink two to three quarts of liquid (preferably water) every day to flush out the chemo and keep the kidneys functioning since some of these medications are hard on the kidneys. Because I didn't want to count wrong, I went and purchased one of those 32 oz. water bottles (BPA free, of course, just in case!) and proceeded to drink two of those each day filled with water, in addition to whatever other liquids I consumed.

Besides the dizziness that first morning after treatment, I also spent most of the day traveling back and forth to the bathroom. Not only did I dump fluids, but also my bowels evacuated about hourly. I couldn't eat a thing because my stomach was essentially full all the time! By the next morning I had lost eight pounds. I woke up with a headache, and had a mild one most of the day. But in my effort to be faithful to my treatment regime, I continued the fluid intake, along with the restroom exercise. I began to develop abdominal pain, ringing in the ears, and by the weekend, I was feeling hopeless and weepy and wondered if I would be able to stand four to six sessions of chemo.

I can only imagine the nurse practitioner's conversations around the office following my desperate phone call to her on Monday morning. I reported the quantities of fluid I had been downing and her first response was an emphatic, "Oh, no!" She said I only need to drink eight cups of liquid, any kind of liquid except caffeinated beverages. That's less than half of what I was putting down, making myself sick, sick, sick, and dehydrated. I suspect I threw my electrolytes way out, too. I started feeling better the very next day, after 24 hours of normal fluid consumption including Gatorade® with saltine crackers.

At my next visit, my oncologist explained that the original research on fluid consumption was not restricted to water only. She reminded me that there are fluids in lots of foods–think spaghetti sauce and pudding, just to name two. I hesitate to estimate exactly how much water I was using to basically poison myself: hydro-poisoning, I suppose it was. At least I know if I ever want to lose a lot of weight fast …. Oh, never mind. I could kill myself that way, as some people have unfortunately done. I'll just stay fluffy.

Crackers, Anyone?

Andrew and I went to the builder's home design center yesterday to select carpet for the new basement room in the townhouse which is being finished before we close. This was shortly after I had the conversation with my nurse practitioner about fluids. I was still feeling a little queasy from my accidental attempts to drown myself, and maybe a little bit queasy from the chemo. I quickly learned that saltine crackers still work their magic, just like they did when I was pregnant. So I carry some on days I'm not feeling my best. Just before we walked in, I ate a few crackers. Then, we went inside and met Holly, the designer. She began by apologetically explaining that she is pregnant and feeling queasy, so if she jumps up and rushes out of the room, she promised she would be right back. Of course I assured her I had been there before and resisted the temptation to tell her I'm in a similar boat now … only it is chemicals making me sick and not a baby! But she really had no idea how much I was identifying with her at that moment.

March 22 or 23

Hair Issues Already!

Today I go to the cancer center salon to get a wig. Already my hair feels a bit dry and lifeless, quicker than I had expected such changes. Most women have told me they lose their hair by about the 3rd week, but the literature says it can happen as early as 7 days, so at least I'll be ready if next week finds me bald. I had thought Ward would shave my head for me when it was time, but he admitted last week that he doesn't think he can do it. It must be very hard to watch the woman you love transform before your eyes in not so good ways. Hopefully, some of these external changes will not be permanent, but the obvious ones will not go away. Still I continue to pray that on the other side of this little adventure, we will find blessings we had not anticipated. *Most of all, Lord, make me the woman you intended me to be when you created me in my mother's womb. Perhaps this part of my journey is really the most important lecture you have prepared for me to deliver. Let me be worthy of your high call.*

There's a part of me that just wishes my hair would go ahead and fall out so I can start dealing with it and moving toward the day it will be growing back in. It died, really, the day of chemo, I think. The morning after, I hopped in the shower and began to shampoo my hair like I have done most days of my life since I was old enough to make that choice for myself. But my hair had been transformed. My soft, fine hair felt coarse and stiff. It didn't lather softly in my hands the way it always had before.

And the second surprise came when I tried to style it. It wouldn't curl around the brush, or lay softly around my face. It wouldn't respond to the heating iron either, but just lay flat and rigid. For several days, I struggled to reclaim my normal hairstyle, which I've already cut a little shorter in anticipation of the wig thing. Finally, I realized that a bunch of conditioner rubbed all over my head, and not just on the ends of my hair, as has been my habit all my life, was the key to manageable hair. Thank goodness I discovered that little gem before I went and got a short spiky punk cut!

So with conditioner as my newfound best friend, I've made peace with my hair and am once again hopeful that the doctor might be wrong–maybe I'll keep most of my hair after all. It happens occasionally, someone doesn't lose their hair to chemo. It could happen that I'll be one of those lucky ones. But just in case I'm not, just in case I follow the normal path for most chemo patients, I have lots of props: wigs and wiglets, hats, scarves and baseball caps. I may be bald, but I aim to be beautiful, too!

March 25, Thursday

Only One Week?

Last night, Ward looked at me and said, "Has it really been only a week since you got your first chemo? It seems like a very long week!" And he was right. It has felt like a very, very long week, with a range of experiences and emotions, and life lived in between them. I know in a few months, I'll look back on these weeks, and they will seem a distant memory, but for the moment, treatment seems to stretch endlessly before me.

My oncologist and my reconstructive surgeon both tell me that statistics support increased exercise to reduce breast cancer recurrence. So in spite of my hatred of exercise programs, I try to walk 45 minutes each day. This week, I've used shopping as my opportunity to walk around stores–that's getting costly for Ward–but shopping is great therapy for me. I notice that the stores are virtually empty in the mornings so I can shop without worrying about crowds or germs. I own the malls in the morning hours.

Last week, however, the weather was lovely and I took Angel walking every day. Angel is a 14 year-old beagle, not in great health, but she seems to enjoy the walks. I just hope my cure doesn't kill her. At least she will die happy! She loves to walk through the little woods behind the high school near our house. I've avoided that pathway this week since my immunosuppression is at it's lowest and mold and spores can be deadly. But, as long as the wind stays down, I'll take her on a couple of those outings again next week–maybe with a scarf across my face. I'm already wearing big-brimmed hats as part of my sun protection and pretending to myself that I look stylish rather than matronly.

March 26, Friday

Braless, at this Age?

My reconstructive surgeon noticed I was coming in for expansion wearing a bra, especially the underwire one which was stressing my skin. I explained to her that it held the extra padding I needed to look balanced. "You know, you don't **need** to wear a bra. These aren't going anywhere," she said, indicating the temporary skin expanders which pass for breasts for me. I went home and thought about that and thought it seemed a little gross for a woman my age to go braless. Yes, I did that back in the 70s along with nearly every other young woman I knew with 20-something breasts. But this isn't the 70s and it just seemed inappropriate. Never mind that I have perky 20-something breasts again–well, sort of.

And then I purchased a sleeveless, V-neck sundress to wear to my son's university graduation, where I suppose about 15,000 people will be crowded onto the outdoor lawn on a late May day in Virginia. I thought about the heat and humidity, the sun beating down on us for hours. So I tried on my dress this morning without a bra and it feels and looks great! I think I could get used to this new stage in my life–very freeing! I may be the only bald and braless mom there, but if I'm not, I know I'll be in great company. We cancer survivors are a hardy, sometimes bald and braless bunch! Nevertheless, I think the stars of TV's "What Not to Wear" would be very proud of me choosing modern, young, fresh looking clothing to match my new figure. I can't wait to tell my plastic surgeon how exciting it was to put on clothes that fit both the top and bottom of me. For someone who has always had a pear shaped figure, I think I could get used to this hourglass shape.

Wigs, Hats and Hygiene

Thank goodness hats are making a style comeback! I've got to sit for hours in the sun on the university lawn to proudly watch my eldest son graduate. Now that's exciting and I wouldn't trade this day for anything. But it does carry some special challenges for a chemo patient. For one thing, we cannot get sunburned. I'll be slathering on sunscreen hourly. And I must stay hydrated–but that will be everyone's challenge that day, I suppose. I don't think I can take that day in a hot wig, so I've decided to sport a big-brimmed hat, glam earrings and make it a style statement! Most people won't know I'm hiding a bald head under all that hat. I just hope I don't sweat my eyebrows off!

Now that I'm collecting wigs and hats and dramatic earrings, false eyelashes and other make-up to hide the altered physical state I anticipate as a chemo patient, I'm worried that I'll mistakenly be arrested as a plus-size hooker or a transvestite. So far, no matter what I do to my wigs, I still look like a woman in a wig. I feel a little outrageous. One thing's for sure, I'm not going anywhere near the red light district down on Broad Street!

Speaking of wigs, I've discovered some really skanky wig shops in this town! I was given a list of local wig shops and decided that I might like to have two or three on hand, just in case. So I began driving around town trying on wigs. The list had been thoughtfully composed with price ranges indicated and I decided I didn't want to spend much on an item I hoped to only need for a few months. Was I wrong in that line of thought! I quickly discovered that a cheap looking wig on a Styrofoam head also looks cheap on a bald human head. So much for my idea about saving money with cheap wigs! A twenty-five dollar wig looks like last year's Halloween costume drug out of the attic, at least on me. I haven't purchased a back-up wig yet.

Personal hygiene takes on a whole new meaning for a chemo patient. I brush my teeth ever so gently with a toothbrush softened in hot water and I try to brush several times a day after I eat. Then I rinse with warm salt water–like a talisman's potion to ward off the evil mouth sores everyone complains about with chemo. So far, it has worked well, I have no mouth sores, but this is only day eight after chemo.

I have posted bottles of waterless hand sanitizer in every room in the house as well as in my car. They stand like guardians of my compromised immune system. I also carry miniature bottles in my purse, sometimes inadvertently more than one. If I touch a pet, I sanitize my hands. Ward changes the cat litter for me and cleans the empty pet bowls after they eat. Outside my home, I carefully avoid touching any surface: handrails, restroom fixtures, doors, handles. I can open a restroom door with a paper towel, wad it up and toss it neatly into the nearest trash can, even clear across the room!

I wash and sanitize my hands so frequently, I remind myself of some of the obsessive-compulsive patients I took care of as a nursing student. It's a wonder my skin is not sloughing off around my wrist and hands! Dry skin is a huge problem all over my body, not just on my abused hands. I fear I may be mistaken for an alligator walking upright, ready for the tanners, so I apply lotion liberally several times a day to keep the purse and shoe designers away from me. I should have purchased stock in a lotion or soap company before I started on this journey. Before this adventure, I never gave germs a thought. My how times have changed!

March 27, Saturday

Cancer is a Family Affair

People often ask me how Ward is doing and I say, "Fine, as far as I can tell." We don't talk about my condition much, but he is doing everything he can to help me, and anything I request.

However I got a glimpse of just what a toll this situation has taken on him as I was showing him the gourmet candy I purchased for Dave's Easter basket. Yes, I still make an Easter basket for this adult son. He reminds me very clearly that he wants one, and even makes requests for certain kinds of chocolate! I gladly comply, searching for unusual and unique gourmet chocolate designs.

One of the Easter treats I selected for Dave's basket this year was a chocolate lollipop on a stick, a pair of brown bunny ears molded tightly together with pink icing coloring the inside of the ears. Ward looked at that chocolate confection kind of funny, and said, "Do you know what that is?"
"Of course I do, don't you?"
"Well, I'm not sure," he said.
"It's bunny ears, Ward, what did you expect? It's Easter!"
He looked relieved and sheepishly admitted that he thought I had mistakenly purchased a piece of joke candy representing a part of a woman's anatomy–and not the Dolly Parton's either! But he couldn't understand why I would buy that for our son!

I burst out laughing. "I'm sorry, honey, it's been a long time, hasn't it?"

Obviously my impaired health has put a bigger strain on his sexual/mental health than I had realized. Bless his heart and I'll try to bless the rest of him soon. I have spent a lot of time laughing about his confusion. I find myself thinking about that initial confused look on his face and his delicate line of questions, and I burst out laughing right out loud! I can be driving down the road and just laugh out. Thank goodness in this day and age, people just assume you are on the cell phone with someone.

This did, however, present the opportunity for us to talk at dinner last night about our current life issues. He admitted that when I am doing well, he is, too. If I'm sad or worried, then he is, too. Unintentionally, that puts a lot of pressure on me to be positive and upbeat so I won't worry him. I know he didn't mean it that way; still, that's how it feels to me. I'll just keep writing and praying because I know God is big enough to handle my anxieties and then some. Regardless of my frame of mind, most of the time, Ward is hopeful and looking forward to the best possible outcome, a complete cure. Besides, he reminded me that early on this journey, God gave him a Bible verse, Ephesians 1:2 "Grace and peace to you from God our Father and the Lord Jesus Christ". It's a simple verse, but Ward didn't know that verse. He was just praying and felt the Spirit whispering "Ephesians 1:2" to him over and over. When he looked it up, he felt God had given him a personal promise of grace and peace from God and from our Lord Jesus Christ–hope for complete healing for the woman he loves: That's ME! Ward clings to the lifeline of those promises, and I know our God is able to give grace and peace abundantly, in any situation. I believe this is the second time God has sent a message to me, a prophecy some would call it. I just know that God keeps speaking peace and hope to me through others.

Comparing War Stories!

"Don't ask, don't tell." This phrase has taken on new meaning as I have realized that being a breast cancer patient is a lot like being pregnant. Everyone wants to compare stories and scare themselves and me to death. If I am talking with a breast cancer survivor who has chosen a different treatment option than I, she sometimes doubts the pathway she chose, or wonders why her doctor didn't offer her the same options that were offered me. Or I might hear someone talking about their treatment options and I feel a little sad that those same great drugs don't work on my kind of cancer. I've decided that once a treatment decision is done, it is not productive to look back and wish for a different pathway, just like every other life choice. Sometimes well-meaning survivors can be a great source of misinformation or raised anxiety. I am making this my motto: *Look forward with hope, rather than backward with regret. Fix the things you can and leave the rest in God's capable hands.*

There are also parables, which pop up along this journey: "Sugar feeds the cancer." "Have a lumpectomy, save your breast; have a mastectomy, save your life." So I try to minimize my discussion about how I'm feeling, what treatment I'm getting, or what my pathology reports showed. I don't even like to talk about stages and I definitely try to avoid discussion about the positive and negative status and grade of my tumor. I don't want people burying me prematurely and I definitely don't want to see pity in the eyes of everyone who looks at me.

I've also been surprised to discover that some women want a lot of information about my presenting symptoms. "Did you find it on a mammogram?" is the first question out of many women's mouths. "No, I had pain in my breast," I answer. And immediately a scared look comes over their faces and I am pelted with more questions. "My breast hurts sometimes," many women have said. "Do you think it could be cancer?" (I don't know, talk to your doctor.) Or, another common response:

"I thought breast cancer isn't painful." (It isn't usually, but I did read online that breast cancer that presents as painful is usually the more aggressive types.) I found these questions a bit frustrating until I mentioned it to another mature friend of mine. "They're scared," she said. "They're afraid they might miss the symptoms." I think she's right.

Sometimes I get a little scared, too, because my cancer is an aggressive type and my statistical chances of survival are less hopeful than many other types of breast cancer. As I understand it, even though I'm a Stage One with no node involvement, my kind of cancer is stealth. It can seed without the typical signs of spreading. Just like the melanoma. So I take the chemo, pray for the best, but ultimately trust the Lord God to order my days according to his Book of Life.

In quiet, alone moments, I sometimes get a little wave of sadness, not fear, but almost a sense of the inevitable, that I'm a short-timer on this earth. I imagine what it will be like those last months if I have to say goodbye to my three men, my elderly dad, my sweet niece, my cherished nephew. And then I make myself stop. These thoughts aren't productive, or healing, or hopeful. I don't know my future and my passing may have no relationship to cancer. So I shut down this unproductive line of thinking and redirect my attention to matters of the moment. Now where did I put those saltine crackers?

March 30, Tuesday

Bye-Bye Hair

My hair started falling out today. I woke up and went into the bathroom for my usual morning routine. My hair was sticking out all over, like I had slept on my head, spinning, all night. I combed through my unruly mop with my fingers and was surprised, but not shocked, to see several strands of hair between my fingers. I hurried back to my pillow, but it was clean. I combed through again–more hair. I looked on the bathroom floor where I had been standing–more hair. Not lots of it, maybe a dozen strands total lying there. But that was a dozen more than had ever fallen out together before. So it begins.

I have read that lots of women shave their heads as soon as the hair starts falling out. It makes them feel more in control of the situation. I, however, have decided that I'd rather go to a pixie cut and see how long it actually takes to go bald. I'm thinking if I can get by for a few more weeks with some hair to peek out from under hats or scarves, I'll feel a little more normal than being totally bald. At some point, when more than 50% of my hair is gone, I may take razor to head, but I'll know when it is time to do that. For the moment, I have an appointment with a hairdresser tomorrow to get a pixie cut. For me, it will be easier to have shorter pieces falling out, I think. While I'm still looking relatively normal, I can't see any point in shaving off all my hair. But once I look patchy or severely thinning, there will be time to take command. And besides, why shouldn't those tenacious little hairs who hang in there be rewarded for their efforts!

Fortunately, I don't have a lot of time to obsess over chemo and its side effects. I have a townhouse purchase to complete and decorate by July 1. I have a son who will be in Blacksburg for the summer, doing summer school, so I have visits to make. After that, my chemo will be done and I'll be busy growing back my own hair. And praying that the cancer is completely gone forever. And getting my chest art completed.

Yesterday was a little hard because I saw a woman who is a cancer survivor who wanted to talk test results and pathology and chemo drugs. I've made a firm pact with myself that I won't talk numbers or treatments with people because it creates anxiety in me. It reminds me how narrow my treatment path is. It shifts my focus from God my Healer to cancer the potential killer. There are some great drugs with excellent treatment successes, but many of them are ineffective for my kind of cancer. I don't like being reminded of the good drugs that aren't available for me. It makes me uncomfortable when someone says "I had the gold standard of treatment" and I'm not getting that one. I trust my oncologist, and I trust my God and my Savior even more. He has ordered my days, and I don't want to compare his choices for someone else to his choices for me. Still, I also don't want to see the look of pity in another person's face when they find out how narrow my treatment options are. God and I are still a majority against cancer cells, and I must keep my focus clearly on him. In fact, he's a majority against my cancer cells, even if I collapse under the weight of the battle.

Besides, I'd much rather talk about dealing with balding or nausea … we all have choices in how we approach those things we can control, and I can control my reaction to side effects. In fact, I've been very blessed. My side effect have been few and minimal so far. I hope this pattern holds out, but more than that, I pray God will give me grace for the moment, whatever the moments hold for me. And I know that he will, because he is my Good Shepherd. *I love you, Lord, for letting me feel positive and hopeful, even on the day that my hair is deciding to abandon me.*

Speaking of weight, I'm still a bit offended that most women gain weight during chemo treatment, rather than lose weight. All my life, I've battled weight gain, and now, when there should be some small pleasure in chemo, losing weight may not be one of them. In fact for the past few days, I've been in a perpetual state of hunger. Yesterday I put myself on a 2–3 hour feeding schedule, like a preemie, hoping if I plan to feed myself healthy food every couple of hours, I won't find myself out and about grabbing junk food to fill my growling stomach. I guess when my body revs up into high gear to rebuild the good cells chemo has destroyed, my metabolism must kick into high gear demanding fuel for the task at hand. So, I'm trying to keep good sources of protein going down the hatch and hope it is put to good use, and not stored as additional pounds on a balding 60 year old! I really, really don't need more pounds!

Chapter 4: APRIL
Hair Trauma

April Musings

Ward and I went to the beach for a long weekend the first weekend in April, which also was Easter weekend. We attended worship services at the local church there in North Myrtle beach where we had worshiped on other Easters that found us at the beach. We came home on the 6th for my second chemo treatment the following day. In some ways the month passed like a whirlwind as I worked on the details of closing the deal on the townhouse, adjusted to my new normal as a chemo patient, and in general learned to cope with the very different lifestyle that treatment imposed upon me. Still, it was a month of blessings and God-shaped surprises.

One enduring memory I will cherish, although I can't remember the exact date, is of a friend who came to visit when she and her husband returned from wintering in Florida. She brought with her pictures she had painted while there. It was a delightful treat for me to see the beautiful canvases Anne created while she was away. I never knew she was a painter, but more importantly, Anne's thoughtful preparation for this visit meant that we had something fun to talk about that had nothing to do with cancer. In my little world reduced to avoiding germ-infested environments, Anne brought a delightful new dimension to my cloistered surroundings. Thank you, Anne!

April 4, Sunday

Easter Sunday in the South

I had forgotten that going to church in the south can be deadly if one is immunosuppressed. Before we even made it into the sanctuary today, one of the choir members rushed out a side door, choir robe flying back as he hurried toward us with outstretched arms. He squeezed me in a big bear hug, which nearly knocked my hat off my head. I think it was his attempt to kiss me that actually tilted the hat. I had hoped that if I did not extend my hand to the gentleman who rushed to greet us on the sidewalk, then a verbal greeting and smile would suffice, but I was wrong. Subtle body language on my part failed to communicate my intention to keep a distance, and I believe had I not been wearing a big hat, he would have planted a kiss right on my face. I'll have to remember to wear a bigger hat next time. It will serve as a barrier to overly friendly folks. I frankly don't want anyone touching me right now because the least little infection can turn dangerous for me, at the least delaying my treatment and even landing me in the hospital–or grave.

Once in the worship center, we chose our seats carefully. We sat at the end of a row near the door where we could make a quick exit without having to shake hands and greet people. So, my only challenge was the greeting during the service, and I had unfortunately left my hand sanitizer at the condo. I'm sure I must have appeared to those around me to be a standoffish, snobby stranger. When someone nearby coughed, I snuggled closer to Ward as though he could keep the germs away.

But my cautious behavior has convicted me of the times I have judged other people's behavior in a less than kind way, assuming the worst, when in fact they may have been someone coping with a challenging situation, just as I am today. How often have I wondered why someone would rush out of church, or sit on the back row, or avoid contact with others? Maybe they were cold or stuck up I might have assumed in the past. But now, I consider other options: Maybe they were ill, or sad, or afraid. Maybe their bodies or they mind or emotions had betrayed them, and they were dealing with a hard situation in the best way that they could. It is so easy to rush to judgment with such scant information. *Lord, help me be mindful that most of us are getting through this life the best we can. And forgive me when I have judged others–that's your job, not mine!*

I find my emotions are sometimes tender and near the surface, as they were this morning at the sunrise service and again as some of the church music was played or sung. I remember that first Easter service after my sister, Catherine, died. Gayton Baptist still met in a school back then, and the setting at church today was in the new family life center, which reminded me of that service in 1992. Back then, when the resurrection songs began, I began to cry and I believe I wept through most of that service. I remember that the pastor's wife called me that afternoon and we went walking as she offered words of comfort and a listening ear. It wasn't the grief of one hopeless, but the awareness that my sister celebrated Easter that year for the first time in the very heavenly presence of our Lord and Savior–and I missed her terribly, even as I knew she was having the Easter of her life!

Today, the songs of victory over the grave and resurrection celebration reminded me that I may be walking closer to eternity than I thought I was a few short months ago. I don't know if I'll beat this cancer or if it will beat me and there are precious few people who know that my cancer can still take me out. After all, it was stage one, no node involvement, but the pathology is a bit more challenging than many cancers, and I have some years to make before I'll know if this thing is beat.

Still, I'll live the number of years, days and hours which the Lord God has assigned to me, and when I slip into those momentary thoughts of uncertainty, I remind myself that "The Lord is my strength and my salvation, whom shall I fear?"[1] "You will not fear ...the pestilence that stalks in the darkness, nor the plague that destroys at midday."[2] The Psalmist's words remind me that God is very capable of handling anything. Surely he can direct these cancer cells in the way he wants them to go–I'm just hoping he's directing them out of me! And as Paul so beautifully wrote in Romans 8, nothing can separate me from the love of God, which is in Christ Jesus my Lord.

April 5, Monday

Hair Today, Gone Tomorrow

My hair is coming out liberally now and I have new sympathy for my dog and cat who shed all over the house every spring. Except that I think shedding is a good thing for them, but for me this will keep going until I am totally bald. And let's face it, even a wet cat looks horrible, much less a bald one, so I'm not expecting much as a skinhead woman!

I don't think Ward has much sympathy for my dilemma; when I mention going bald, he just says, "Tell me about it!" But I know for a fact it took him years to get bald and he still has some hair. At this rate, I'm going to be totally bald within a few days or a week! I'm accomplishing in a few days something that he has been working on for a long, long time. But honestly, I do have

1   Psalm 27:1

2   Psalm 91

the reasonable hope of getting hair back eventually, when the chemo is done and my poor bald head has the chance to grow back some hair. Ward's only hope, outside of a miracle, is that somebody finally develops a drug which will grow hair back– and I'm not talking about Rogaine® either, which was a costly bust in Ward's case twenty-some years ago.

My hair started coming out last Tuesday and today I'm wearing a hat all day to control the fallout. Otherwise I leave a trail of fallen hair everywhere I go, even when I'm sitting still. I know many women just shave their heads when they get to this point, but honestly, there's a part of me that wants to see exactly how this plays out. I think I'm secretly still hoping that I'll keep a little hair, just a little fluff along the neckline and at the ears would be a welcome treat, but I'm pretty sure that is not to be. At any rate, I'll enjoy what little bit stays for the next few days anyway. And I'll control the flyaway hair (new meaning for that term!) with hats and scarves and the wig in waiting.

My longtime friend, Kate, wrote me a sweet email Friday comparing me with her brother, Pete, whom she adores and who has been battling a rare form of anemia which looks like and is treated like cancer–bone marrow transplants and severe immunosuppression have been treatments which Pete has experienced. I was flattered, and humbled, that Kate would compare me to Pete; I think of him as a giant of a man mentally and spiritually. It seemed odd to see my name beside his in such a complimentary way. Pete's battle has gone on for years, and I've only been in this one since January. Nevertheless, I'm honored to be considered worthy of the comparison; I am more honored still that the Lord God would give me the privilege to serve him all these years–and who knows if this is my most challenging and most rewarding assignment yet.

Regardless, I do know this: *I want to live, Lord God, in such a way that I will bring you honor and glory, and point many people* to Jesus, regardless of whether my time here on Earth is long or short, or somewhere in between. *Honestly, on this side of sixty, it can't be as long as it has been anyway, so Lord, help me enjoy the ride, wherever it takes me. At the end of the day, more than anything else, let me live so that those I love will be left with a legacy that solidifies their relationship with Christ. I just want to enjoy heaven with my sons, my husband, my loved ones there with me.*

Blessings in Skin

I continue to be amazed by the people God has put along my pathway to make this journey easier. I remember a lady I met in the waiting room at the hospital the morning I waited to be escorted into the surgical area. She struck up a conversation with me about the Sudoku puzzle I was working but it quickly moved to the reasons we were there. She was having knee surgery and she seemed surprised to hear my diagnosis (it's easier to tell to a stranger). She offered words of encouragement and promises to pray for me and I suspect she did.

Then there's Donna, a cosmetologist who runs a free wig salon ministry at the cancer center. She fits ladies like myself who are facing hair loss. She spent two hours with me, as though she had the rest of her life to get me fitted into a wig in which I will feel comfortable. She also taught me about wig care and showed me lots of ways to tie a scarf. In fact, she also taught me how to convert a tee shirt into a charming turban. I left her shop clutching a stylish wig and a head full of new ways to cope with a bald pate.

Next there was Cheryl. I learned about Cheryl through a card and note from Sally, who had been a Fellowship of Christian Athletes mom with me way back when our boys were in middle school. When she heard I had cancer, she wrote a note telling me about her hairdresser who helps cancer patients with hairstyles and wigs. When my hair started jumping ship last Tuesday, I dug through the drawer of cards and letters sent to me during this illness, and found Sally's note. Then I called her hair dresser, Cheryl, who made room for me the next day. She cut me a cute short haircut so I would be less traumatized as it began to go. It's a cut similar to the wig Donna gave me, so the transition will be less startling. And surprise, surprise! I actually really liked the short style. That made me much less anxious about the growing out process. I was thinking I'd be in a wig forever, but now I know when I have just a couple of inches of hair, I can get it styled and tuck the wig back in the closet where I hope I'll never have to wear it again for baldness!

But I'll tuck it back gently, with the hope that in a few years, I can donate it to some other outlet where maybe another woman can be blessed with a change of wigs as she moves toward health and life as I am doing now. I'm also expecting God to give me a ministry of service for these next years–perhaps in cancer care, but maybe in some other arena. *The fields are white unto harvest, but the laborers are few.*[3] *Show me, Lord, what kind of labor you have prepared for me next.*

April 7, Wednesday

Second Round of Chemo

I'm at the infusion center for my second chemo treatment and am encouraged that the nurse says I'm not likely to develop side effects beyond what I had this last time. Piece of cake! I worked like crazy yesterday at the condo, packing away for the summer, adding new mattress and box spring covers. It really looked beautiful when I was done. Ward also helped a lot this time with the cleaning and putting away of our personal belongings. He always does his part, but some of the dirtier stuff he had to

3   John 4:35

do without me this time. He cleaned all the bathrooms, floors, and emptied the vacuum–things I normally do.

Yesterday was the shocker day of realizing that I've lost most of my hair now. Of course it was not a big surprise; I've been collecting it in baggies to experiment with wig making. It would be an easier process had I left it long, but it would also have been a more shocking one. I figure the longer the hair when it falls, the more noticeable the transition. With the short haircut Cheryl did for me last week, I actually lost a lot without looking conspicuous. But yesterday, it looked pretty bad and I wore my wig for the first time to go out to dinner with Ward. I told him I am ready to cut the rest of it off and asked him if he was still hesitant to shave it for me. "No," he said. "I can do it now; I just didn't think I could do it when it was long and full." I suspect at this point he is as tired of seeing hair all over the place as I am, so cutting the rest off wouldn't be traumatic for either of us. In fact, I was kind of tired of hair down my back, on my clothes and occasionally in my mouth or caught on lipstick, and occasionally in my contacts as I tried to put them in. Do you know how painful a little skinny hair can be caught between the contact and the eyeball?

Therefore when we arrived back in Richmond about midnight, we pulled out the home clipper set. We attached the shortest clipper guard and he went right to shaving. Now I have quarter inch head stubble. Being the vain gal that I am, I left about a two-inch fringe at the bottom back, and what's left of the side burns in front of my ears. It's pretty thin there, but I'm clinging to the few hairs that are left which give me a little something to hang out of hats.

Speaking of hats! How do these men walk around in hats 24/7? I'm about to die from heat! I have straw hats, sun hats that look like a southern belle from the 1800s, and baseball caps, as well as a couple of tams and a bucket hat or two. Some look a little more flattering than others, and I'm especially eager to try the tee-shirt turban, which Donna at the cancer center salon taught me to tie. It's rather ethnic looking, but I may be able to pull it off with big skirts and wild earrings.

I realized yesterday, I'm in a surreal place. I am rapidly losing hair, I put bras onto fake breasts, which refuse to fill them out, even though I have pretty good volume, but it's bound tightly by muscle. I must remember to ask my plastic surgeon some questions about ultimate shape, etc. I know she doesn't want me to wear underwire, so I'm going to cut those out of the dozens of bras I currently own, all purchased to fit my ill shaped previous real breasts. Funny the number of women who have talked to me since my diagnosis and surgery expressing dissatisfaction with their shape, and I have been one of those most of my life. Now I'm stuffing cotton into bras, popping wigs on my head, and carefully watching a toe I stubbed hoping I'm not developing toenail problems. What efforts to feel like I look normal! I got my toes Frenched and I keep my fingers that way, too, as acrylics and I'm hoping that I can continue this process throughout the treatment. So for a rapidly transforming body, I look pretty good when I'm all dolled up! But it is a surreal existence right now.

I got a cute email from our church secretary yesterday in response to one I sent her. Lyn is a very encouraging woman in her quiet caring way. I had updated her on my hair loss– funny how much that occupies my time and thought process– more so than my altered chest, or the cancer that was there. I suppose that's because everyone can see the wig and other accoutrements, but the fake boobs and cotton are known only to me and Ward (and anyone who might eventually read this account). At any rate, Lyn said, "After your hair grows out, you'll never have a bad hair day again, because even the worst hair day is still hair!" It's funny how life redefines our frame of reference sometimes. And that's a good thing, or we might never grow spiritually or mentally or emotionally. *I must*

remember to be thankful, God, for the lessons along this way
which I might not have learned on any other pathway.

My doctor and the nursing staff are so pleased with my
excellent results on this chemo cycle–very mild side effects,
great mental and physical condition, and they are all very
encouraging. I did learn that I'm not getting the same chemo
drugs some of my acquaintances did because the newer trend
is to give drugs with less long-term potential for permanent
issues, like heart disease. The two I'm on do require a three-
week cycle because they have a longer T-time, so that's okay
with me. (That's T-time, not tee time, golfers, but a measure
of the time it takes the drug to break down and clear from the
body.) My doctor will adjust my treatment schedule for my son's
university graduation, and that's a good thing for me. I really
love my doctor–all of them actually, I feel very blessed to have
such a great medical team.

The infusion center where I receive treatment is also the perfect
setting for me–private room, great nurses, and kind volunteers.
There's a TV in each room but I mostly read or use Ward's
laptop. I guess if I were an animal, I'd be a big ole bear who
likes to crawl up in her cave and hibernate until the winter
passes. Only it's spring right now in Virginia, my favorite time
of year, and I love the sunshine and flowers. Still, I enjoy getting
medical treatment in the relative privacy of my little room.
I just snuggle into the comfy recliner and lose myself in my
books or web pages.

Ward's sense of humor continues to bless me on this journey
as does his easy acceptance of my altered looks. He often tells
me I look great. Last night, after the haircut, he looked at me
and said, "Well, you have a nicely shaped head." I must have
given him a funny look–nice shaped heads are great for a bald
man, but women don't want to be bald, even if their heads
are nicely shaped. He probably recognized the uselessness of

that comment to a woman, and he started laughing and said, "You know, for a bald woman, you have a nicely shaped head." And we both stood there and laughed silly! I fell in love with Ward at least in part because of his great sense of humor and it continues to sustain me today. *Thank You Lord, that all those years ago, You knew I would need Ward to laugh me through this one! You are always right on time!*

April 12, Monday

Nematodes and Wigs

Andrew came home this weekend to work on a poster for a class in infectious diseases. A poster! He's getting ready to graduate Phi Beta Kappa from UVA, and he had to make a poster. He thinks the last time he made a poster for a class requirement was when he was in middle school. Apparently this professor likes to irritate the department folks by having his students make a poster (for 25% of their grade), and hang them in the hallways on display. So Andrew came home to raid my craft supplies and for artistic consultation–that's fancy for pick mom's brain for creative ideas. It was a unique experience to once again be sitting alongside my son as he cut and colored and pasted construction paper, then typed and glued onto poster board as he had done so many times when he was a little fellow. Now he towers over me by several inches and exceeds me in brainpower beyond my ability to guess.

His project was about the sugar beet cyst nematode, a disgusting little creature that I didn't know existed before this weekend. The short story is that this pest causes millions of dollars in crop damage worldwide each year, but that's not the part that bothered Andrew. Here's the thing that grossed him out: the fertilized eggs continue to grow in the mother as she

feeds them until they kill her, and then her dead body forms
a cyst where the offspring live and grow and wait to start the
lifecycle over again, sometimes after several years. Andrew
has studied lots of hard stuff, dissected numerous creatures as
a biology major, but this really bothered him. I couldn't help
but think that perhaps he sat with his own mother, wondering
if there are errant cancer cells hiding in my body, waiting to
burst forth at some future date to destroy my life. This is an
unanswerable question. We all have to wait and see. In the
meantime, I had a great weekend playing school one more time
with my now grown and very accomplished son.

Andrew and I went shopping Saturday at our giant mall. I
was sporting my new reddish wig which I've affectionately (or
not so affectionately) named The Lucy-Ann: short for a cross
between Lucille Ball and Little Orphan Annie, which is what
I feel like in this curly do. I have two wigs so far: each one
donated by organizations that help chemo patients cope. When
Andrew mentioned that some of his friends might be shopping
there too, I quickly asked, "Do they know I have breast cancer?
I don't want your friends to see me in a goofy wig and think I'm
trying to look like this on purpose!"

Back in the early seventies, cheap wigs were a big fashion item
and I owned several. Many women did, and we popped them
on and off our heads to match our moods. Everyone knew
they were wigs, and everyone else was wearing them, too. I'm
sure we all looked silly–but that's the point: We **all** looked silly.
Now I feel like everyone else looks fine, and I look silly, or like
a pretender. I've discovered by surfing the web that this is a
real problem in the lives of many women of color. Apparently
wigs are a much more popular fashion accessory for African
American women. However, there appears to be a lot of internet
discussion about whether or not one should wear a wig in their
culture, and whether they are pretenders .... yada yada yada.
Aren't we all trying to get through this life the best we can?

This little side adventure reminds me that what we all need is a big dose of grace and mercy toward one another, whatever our color, culture, or hair follicle challenges. It's all a learning process, anyway, and I have learned a lot thus far.

What I've learned about wigs on this journey are these things:

- I have a little head: both of my wigs swallow me.

- I don't have a very prominent back of the head, so there's nothing for my wigs to catch and hold to at the bottom. It rides up like a bad pair of pants.

- The elastic adjustment strips make the wigs tighter around the circumference, but actually don't hold them on any better. It's like a rubber band which continually rolls up. Besides, I have about a half inch to one inch space between scalp and wig. Talk about a big headed look!

- The silicone band I purchased to wear under the wig does cling snuggly to my head. It provides a little more stability to the wig, but a lot more head compression and eventually a headache.

- Wigs are hot, and itchy, and they are supposed to be worn lower on one's forehead than my natural hairline. Feels like a furry stocking cap.

- No matter what I do to the wig, it still looks like a wig, and I feel conspicuous out in public. I feel like everyone is looking at me and thinking, "Who does that woman think she is fooling with that cheap wig!"

Not that I've found a good option yet. Wigs look fake and hats, turbans, scarves all scream "Chemo patient coming through." I mostly opt for scarves or bandanas at home, but when I catch my reflection as I pass a mirror, I see an elderly woman glancing back. Hair does a lot to preserve one's feeling of being younger than one is–in my case, my graying hair disappeared under hair dye years ago, and my glasses were replaced with contacts. In my own mind, I don't look my sixty years. Except that with these tacky scarves and turbans, I think I look about 10 years older!

The lady at one organization taught me how to make a turban out of an old tee shirt, and even how to jazz it up by wrapping a pretty colored scarf around the edges. It is a cute idea, an easy one, and comfortable. But it has an ethnic look, and so when I see myself in it, I think I look like an elderly anemic African queen. Big earrings reinforce the image! It's funny that I've lost two boobs, may be in a losing battle with breast cancer, but I am most distressed about being bald–a temporary condition which will be resolved in several months. I suppose that's God's way of getting my focus off of the issues I can't do anything about and giving me a place to stew over a small, but inconsequential, life event.

In fact, I can't do anything substantive about the hair loss either! I'm just practicing damage control. Yesterday, Ward drove his parents to North Carolina to check on the country house which was my mother-in-law's family home place. Andrew went to a shooting range with his fraternity, and I sat at home carefully gluing hair–my real hair–onto two strips of lace. You see, I got the bright idea, as my hair started falling out, that I should save it and see if I could at least fashion some bangs from it to peek out from under a hat or scarf. But most of it didn't come out in neat little clumps. Instead it fell out hair by hair. Since it is chemically colored, the roots are dark, so not only did I have to sort the hairs into straight little lines, but they had to be turned the right direction. I spent most of the day sorting and gluing, but at the end of the day, I have lightweight bangs from my real hair, which is much finer than synthetic or even commercial human hair. When I affix those bangs to my headdress, I think

I look more like me smiling back in the mirror. When Andrew came home and I told him what I'd been doing, he laughed and said, "I wondered what all those little baggies of hair were all over the house." Now he knows.

And Ward thought it looked great. Or at least that's his story to me. I fear he would tell me anything to make me feel good about my appearance, so I've made him promise to be honest when I say, "Honey, how does this look?" We are way past the classic comedy question between wives and husbands, "Does this make me look fat?" No, my question is, "Does this make me look stupid?" I can deal with fat, but I don't want to look like a freak.

April 13, Tuesday

Adapting to Changes

The wig issue continues to bug me. I went out shopping yesterday in The Lucy-Ann. In the grocery store, I passed a friend who looked right at me and did not see me–no hint of recognition on her face. Now, this disguise could have its usefulness. I could get away with a lot of outrageous behavior incognito. I could even develop an alternate personality–how fun could that be! But actually, I already do pretty much what I want to do as my real self–I don't need to hide behind a false identity. And I'm finding it a little bit lonely underneath the wig. I don't even recognize myself.

I know that I don't have to choose the level of isolation I am living–so different from my normal life–but I continue to believe that carefully guarding my exposure to potential germs is the right thing for me. I also permit myself the luxury of being as lazy as I want to be, within reason. I'm getting exercise each day as my doctors have encouraged, but I sit down or lay down as often as I want to on these tiring days. I'm working really hard to listen to my body and obey its demands. I try to eat the things my body is craving, rest when it says, "I'm tired" and go and do things when I have energy. Indigestion has been a more frequent companion this time around, and Tums are becoming my new best friend. For a woman who rarely used any medication a few months ago, I'm getting to be an expert at popping over-the-counter pills and potions.

Avoiding my usual circle of friends is probably also a defense mechanism of sorts. Many people are so concerned about me that it becomes almost a burden to be around caring folks. They ask many questions, some of which I don't want to talk about. They express their own worry about me and it becomes tiring to try to alleviate their anxiety. I remember a family member who called me early on. The conversation went something like this:

"Carolyn, how are you doing?"

"I'm great. How are you?"

"Well, I'm fine, but I'm just so worried about you!"

What am I supposed to do with that comment? I've now become a person who is causing her additional worry and burden. I didn't choose this role, it was thrust upon me, and I don't have the emotional energy to take responsibility for the mental health or stress of others right now. I'm not comfortable with free-floating anxiety bouncing all around me. So I avoid people I know all together.

Cancer creates an awkward circle around its victim, an artificial bubble that people feel they must wade through each time they see me. I don't want to have to acknowledge my cancerous condition each time I see someone. I hate the expressions of sorrow that I've gotten cancer–I often feel like I am attending my own wake when people come rushing toward me with hugs and expressions of sympathy and a pitiful whine in their voice. I may be buried in a few years, but I'd like to wait for the sympathy until it is warranted. In the interim, I wish this were just treated like a broken leg or something. I do plan to get over this, too, even if my cure turns out to be temporary. Technically, I was cured of cancer when surgery was complete and chemo is a precaution to hopefully kill any little seed cells that might have escaped before the surgery. Only time will tell. In the meantime, I just want to live fully and with hope, not draped in sadness or mourning or sympathy. I want to be seen as Just Carolyn, but I fear for the rest of my life I will live as "*Carolyn-She-Had-Breast-Cancer-You-Know.*"

I've already mentioned that I was divorced when I was young. Back when it happened, there was still quite a societal stigma attached to being divorced at any age, and I didn't want to be Carolyn-the-divorcee. I didn't want to be considered different, or damaged, or not quite as acceptable as others. So I guarded my secret with tenacity. Now I have a different label and I fear I won't be able to escape it. Carolyn-With-Cancer. It has a certain poetic tone, but I still just want to be Carolyn. Carolyn with nothing. Just Carolyn.

I'm so much more than a cancer diagnosis or a chemo patient. I'm still a mom, a wife, a friend, a woman of God. I'm busy buying a townhouse and helping my son prepare to move into it. I'm occupied with Andrew's upcoming graduation. I'm excited about Dave's hard work in college and his own excitement about the coming year in his new living arrangement with some of his Christian brothers at Virginia Tech. I'm thinking about what furniture of his will be used in their new townhouse in Blacksburg, and which furniture might find a new home on Cary Street with Andrew. I still have projects to complete, thoughts to organize into a family history, a book or two begging writing. I can't stand pity! And I won't be wrapped in someone else's anxiety–that mantle is too heavy for me.

I used to teach a women's retreat about dealing with change. I'd faced a lot of changes in my life; thought I'd learned how to make lemonade from life's lemons. But now I'm not so sure. This is a mighty big lemon and I'm not sure I'm up to the task. Fortunately, I know the One who is up to the task, and I must remember to run to him every time I am frustrated with this call. I am confident God has called me to this journey and he will accompany me through it. I wanted to be a missionary when I was younger. I envisioned ministry in foreign lands. Well, I'm in foreign territory now. I must remember that God placed me in this place, perhaps "for such a time as this," just like he called Esther to the pagan king's court. Cancer is a pagan king, but God my Savior is King of Kings and Lord of Lords. He's also Lord over the cancer cells. I must keep my focus upon him, and shake off the well-intended labels the world would place on my life. To God, I'm still just Carolyn, and he is still my precious, gracious, merciful, sovereign Lord. I must keep a clear head about me in this strange place and keep my eyes on Jesus. He's been here before, he knows the lay of the land, and he will light my path one step at a time. I need no more than that. *Forgive me Lord, when I am frustrated with the awkward attempts of others to comfort me; they mean well and they're walking in a strange land, too.*

April 14, Wednesday

Last night, as I prepared for bed, I noticed I have become Carolyn-of-The-Velvet-Mouth, or suede, maybe. The roof of my mouth has a rough texture and feels a little dry, not wet, smooth and slippery like a normal mouth. I remember, now, that my mouth felt exactly this way at this point in my chemo cycle last time. It went away in a few days, and frequent, gentle brushing of teeth plus mouthwashes with warm salt water helped me feel more comfortable. Not that there's any pain with it, but it's sort of like a broken tooth; your tongue wants to keep rubbing the foreign spot, as though checking over and over will eventually reveal that all is normal. Well, as one of my favorite writers, Patsy Clairmont, said, "Normal is just a setting on the dryer" and that's never been truer in my life than now! So for the next few days, normal for my mouth is a palate clothed in sweaters.

Lord God, I have a confession to make. All through this cancer journey, you have poured out your mercy and grace upon me. You have made my pathway easy, and I can celebrate with the Psalmist: "Lord, You have assigned me my portion and my cup; You have made my lot secure. The boundary lines have fallen for me in pleasant places; surely I have a delightful inheritance."⁴ My boundary lines have fallen in pleasant places, Lord. The surgery was less traumatic than I expected, my recovery was swift. The cellulitis which developed and required another week in the hospital was not painful, the hospitalization was easy in a nice facility. I did not lose my implants. Chemo has gone very well, my side effects are minimal, and my recovery from each cycle is strong. I feel great most of the time. I am happy, I'm at peace, I am enjoying life–except for missing my friends, and in a way, I'm enjoying my hermit-like existence, even. I'm looking at this as a sabbatical sort of. I write, I think, I rest. I don't do that very often in my usual life! Surely you have caused my boundary lines to fall in pleasant places.⁵

But here's the confession part. I keep hedging in my mind whether or not I am healed. I want to be, but I'm afraid to say that I am. After all, lots of strong Christian women die from breast cancer every year. I know there is a 15% chance of recurrence of my type, and so there's a little part of me that keeps wanting to protect myself from future disappointment should I be one who does not survive this disease. I'm permitting that little corner of doubt to remain in my heart, a protection against the fear that in your

---

4   *Psalm 16:5-6*

5   *Psalm 16:6*

sovereign plan for my life, I will have metastasis down the road. I want to be faithful to you, and I also want to represent you faithfully to others. I dare not assume that you will not let this cancer return or that I am in any way more deserving of long life than any of my sweet sisters who have gone before me, ushered into your presence by the ravages of cancer.

So please help me, Lord and Father, to get the proper perspective in my thoughts. Help me to live like I'm going to reach 100, but also be prepared to enter eternity tomorrow. I think that's every Christian's call. Help me to live hopefully and most importantly, as a living witness to your great love for your children. I remember clearly a couple of years ago when I made a terrible driving mistake. I pulled into the path of an oncoming car whose driver swerved hard and braked harder, missing me on the driver's side by inches. I was shaken for weeks after that, very much aware that you snatched me from the jaws of death. Our family went on vacation a few days later, and I remember walking with my husband and sons aware that they could have easily been standing over my grave instead of strolling carefree with me down the beach. Help me, Lord, to put cancer out of my mind and live with joy each moment. Remind me that all of my moments are yours and my life is yours to do with as you please. How can I be disappointed in whatever pathway you select? It will all be good.

Michelle, my sweet Michelle, my champion, my soul sister, spoke strong words of encouragement to me yesterday, and once again, I believe this was a prophecy from you, Lord. She said, "Carolyn, when I pray for you, I always get a strong sense of peace. I feel very positive about your outcome and I do not believe the cancer is coming back. I think it's gone, because every time I think of you in prayer, I feel peace, nothing else, just peace." Lord, Michelle's words reminded me of Pat's words of encouragement from you that first week as I waited and wondered if I was a short-timer. As long as I live, I will see Pat climbing up those sound booth stairs to speak words of life: "Carolyn, I just have a strong sense that everything is going to be all right." Your waves of peace swept over me at that moment when Pat spoke, and for the first time that week I had hope and peace in place of the overwhelming waves of sadness. I ate food for the first time that week, lunch with my CBS sisters, and the next day, my biopsy came back breast cancer–not melanoma. I had a chance to live.

Last night, Michelle's words confirmed those of Pat. I'm going to be just fine. I can quit waiting for the other shoe to drop. I can complete this course with joy and look forward to the rest of my life. You are good, God. You are great, and gracious. You will cause my boundaries to fall in pleasant places, for surely I have a delightful inheritance in you. What more could I ask? And one more word of thanksgiving, God. Thank you for putting Michelle in my life. I know you didn't move her to Richmond just for me, but you surely have blessed me because she is in my life. And thank you for the amazing testimony you have built into her life. The incredibly healing of her hand, following a freak accident, which confounds doctors and therapists, is medically incomprehensible. But you are the great physician! Help her surgeon to recognize that there is life in Christ and not in any other! Thank you for giving me the privilege to watch that miracle from the sidelines. I also thank you that Michelle gets my struggle with dealing with labels and pity. Okay, God, so that's more than one more thing. But you have done so much for me and this short list doesn't even graze the surface. You are my awesome God! Therefore, Lord, help me live victoriously and not with trepidation.

When the diagnosis of cancer comes along, one's world is immediately turned cockeyed. In my case, as I looked forward to the coming months, I anticipated certain things would happen, and they did not, and I did not foresee some things that fortunately others who had gone before anticipated for me. One simple example: the need for a journal. I'm a big journaler; I have bound books of blank paper all over my house. In fact,

I immediately grabbed one to start listing gifts and food that poured into this house for me, as well as flowers to the hospital and home. That way, I could be sure I got thank you notes out. About the time I was admitted for the infection, I started another journal listing drugs and side effects and accumulated quite a list in those six days.

But early in my adventure, the women of the church tied a prayer blanket for me. Tucked into the bag in which it was delivered was a hand assembled journal–which included a calendar, and tabs for several sections with topics like:

- Appointments

- Medications

- Questions and Answers for Doctors

- Doctors

There were also blank tabs in the front so I could add additional sections, and I added a lot. Nursing notes, medication reactions, health history, to name a few. This tool became invaluable to me, because at every new doctor visit (and I collected more doctors than I'd dreamed), they wanted my entire health history, including names, phone numbers, fax numbers and addresses of all doctors who have treated me: gynecologist, internist, cardiologist, and other surgeons. These were added to the list of docs I acquired in January and February: oncologists, general surgeon, reconstruction surgeon, infectious disease doctor, radiologists. For a while, I seemed to be going to some doctor every other day–what a social life! Yet in all of this collection of doctors, and places, and treatments, I just kept documenting in the handy journal.

I quickly learned to carry it with me no matter where I went–even to the beauty salons to get wigs! That notebook looked like a simple little spiral collection of paper when I pulled it out of that gift bag, but it has become an indispensable tool for me. I've affectionately named it "My Paper Brain" and I'm careful to always know where it is. I joke that I got "chemo brain" well before my first infusion, but honestly, the diagnosis of cancer scrambled my brain cells, I'm sure, and my paper brain has helped give order and organization to my trail to health. I'm so thankful that Mary Anne tucked that little journal into my gift bag. She's a church member who had walked this journey ahead of me, anticipated the need I didn't even know I had, and met it before I knew to ask. God has done that for me all along the way, and I am grateful.

Fast showers

I used to wonder how my husband could get in and out of the shower in such a short amount of time and still get everything washed. Now I know. I can be in and out in 2 -3 minutes and here's how. I no longer have hair to wash, rinse thoroughly, wash again, rinse very thoroughly, condition, wait one minute, rinse thoroughly and wring out excess water. I have no underarm or leg hair to soap down, shave, rinse and moisturize with baby oil. Now I just hop in the shower, soap up my cloth, wash head to toe, rinse and hop out. No hair dryer needed, just dry bald head, pop on wig or hat and go. It's a simple, simple life as a bald girl, and I can't wait to get back to my complicated showers!

I have a few hairs growing back in on top of my head, so I eagerly went to the internet to see if that's normal. Unfortunately, for the drugs I'm on, it is possible for some hair to start growing back in, but not enough to make any difference. Oh, well, I wasn't anticipating hair for several months anyway, so I'll just be amused by these little persistent guys. At least they're trying to do the right thing.

April 15, Thursday

Lisa's Chicken Soup

Today I woke up rested and feeling great! I can feel my energy coming back–I'll bet its Lisa's soup. Dear Lisa makes an amazing all white meat chicken and fresh vegetable soup, which has become a ministry for her to friends who are on chemo. Lisa cooks soup and prays for the recipient–in this case, me! I think it began with Brenda who reached a point in her chemo treatment where she could eat little and the only thing that appealed to her was Lisa's soup. So Lisa would make a batch for Brenda each time she had a treatment. That was some five years ago, and Brenda is still doing great, and told me about Lisa's soup.

When my chemo schedule was announced, Lisa offered me a batch of chicken soup for each treatment, and I decided that the optimum week for me would be when I was at my nadir–the 7 to 10 days post chemo when my body is most immunosuppressed and I am with the least amount of energy. In the midst of repainting her bedroom, which has been completely reconstructed following a ceiling, cave in, Lisa interrupted her work to make me a batch of her great soup. I ate two delicious bowls for dinner and I'll have more for lunch the next few days. I feel like Popeye the Sailor Man, only my spinach is Lisa's healing chicken soup. I am strong! I am well! I could take on the world! Instead, I'm going to take on my dusty house today. I believe I can write my name in the dust on every surface, so it's time to tackle the offending particles before I accidentally make a man. And while I dust, I'll pray, *"Thank you, God, for Lisa's prayer-filled chicken soup!"*

This afternoon, I go to Planet Hair for a wig consultation. I am hoping she can fit me with something I'll be comfortable in. I really can barely stand to go out in the two wigs I have. One looks a little too perfect and I think I look like a dolled up old lady. It looks good but it's not me. The other one is the red *Lucy-Ann*. I can't take another day in that one! Maybe if I owned a dozen I'd still feel the same, but the two I have are pretty inexpensive, and not fitted directly to me, so I'm hoping a custom fit will at least be more manageable. I've got to get past obsessing with my hair, but really, it is such a part of a woman's identity. When friends don't recognize me in public, that's serious! And I feel goofy. There's still that wig over at the plaza which I liked, but I'm hesitant to order one since I wasn't able to zero in on a color I liked and it's hard to anticipate what it will look like sight unseen. Also, their wigs were all stretch, one size fits all, and that makes me a little nervous, since I'm already swimming in one wig I own. I've never been a one size fits all woman on any other part of my body, and I don't think my head is either! Wigs! Wigs! Wigs! I've got to get off of this subject!

Andrew comes home tomorrow for a few hours on his way to Christopher Newport to celebrate his girlfriend Christin's birthday. He got her a cool sweatshirt and a fondue pot. He's taking dinner down there so they can initiate the pot and I'm going to shop with him to gather ingredients. What a throwback! I remember the 70's when fondue pots first hit the scene. Everybody got fondue pots as gifts, including me, and I even had a fondue recipe book, too. Unfortunately that book is long gone; otherwise it would be a fun relic to pass along. For today, I'm eager for a diversion and shopping fondue will be a fun excursion down memory lane.

Ward and I went to a local fondue restaurant once several years ago to celebrate one of our anniversaries–I don't remember which one. But he hated it. For him, cooking one's own dinner, bite by bite was not his idea of a good time. The guy has a great metabolism and when he sits down starving for a good meal, he doesn't want it stretched out over several hours of nibbling morsels of food. I think he totally missed the object of fondue dinners: relaxed conversation and interaction over a leisurely meal. His idea of a great meal is to be served delicious, amazing food prepared by an excellent chef and delivered course by course in a beautiful presentation, like they do at Hondo's or Ruth's Chris or Buckheads. I'm kind of with him on that: sipping wine and talking to the man I love over delectable courses delivered beautifully, and tastefully, is also my idea of a great meal. In fact, when I'm done with chemo, one of the first things I want is a nice rare steak with a salad served with fresh blue cheese dressing and a nice glass of wine–mouth heaven!

I have been surprised by the foods one must avoid when one is immunosuppressed. Proteins, most importantly for me that includes steak, salmon and tuna steaks, must be cooked well-done, also known as shoe-leather-tough in my book. I would never ruin a good steak, hoof or fin, by having it overcooked, so I stick with ordering chicken most of the time when we are out. Honestly, I'm expecting to sprout feathers in place of hair.

Buffets and salad bars are to be avoided, fresh fruits unless they can be peeled; no fresh berries–I love strawberries and blueberries! Blue cheese has a mold vein running through it; that's forbidden. I believe I read that fresh mushrooms are off the eating list, they're a fungus–I've got to check that out again. So, that wipes out most of the foods that are staples in my life. I pop mushrooms and cherry tomatoes like candy, and I'm not sure where cherry tomatoes fall in this food category since they have a skin. I haven't verified all this with my doctor, I suppose I should, but I was given so many resources about dealing with cancer and chemo that carried these various warnings, and I've tried to be faithful to follow them. There are so many germs one doesn't usually think about: like water in fresh flowers, dirt in the flower beds, mold in leaves and mulch, closets or little used rooms which have collected too much ancient dust.

Of course, this could be like the water advice in some of the literature–way over the top and bordering on dangerous if one takes it seriously like I did the first time around. I honestly still laugh at myself nearly drowning me with fluids those first few days after the first chemo. I've always said I am an RN with just enough knowledge to be dangerous, and now I'm living proof of that fact. I really nearly became my own disaster nurse! Oh well, they say "All's well that ends well" and I seem to be doing fine, just fine.

Happy Hair!

Yeah! I've found my happy hair! I no longer feel like a freak. Cheryl at Planet Hair just fitted me with a wig that is comfortable, casual, my color, my style–and I am finally happy with myself again. I look in the mirror and Carolyn smiles back. In fact, I nearly had two rear end accidents because driving from Cheryl's shop, I kept looking in the rear view mirror at myself instead of watching the road. Fortunately, I stopped in time both times. I can just hear it now, "But officer, I just couldn't stop looking at myself in the mirror. I look so good. I've found myself again."

"Yeah, lady, and you found the trunk of that car too. Now let me see your driver's license–you do have one, don't you?"

Now I want to go somewhere. I want to see people. I'd like to walk through a store and have a friend recognize me. Actually, I was so happy with my look I drove from the beauty shop to Ward's office where everyone complimented me. But most importantly, Ward heard the commotion, stepped out of the treatment room and gave me two thumbs up. That made my day. Besides, this wig fits well, is comfortable, lightweight, has movement, and does not scream, "Clear the way, wig coming through!"

Oh, thank you Lord for the small joys of life. In fact, in my life, this is a big one! Thank you, thank you, thank you for caring about the details which concern me. And I promise, now that I don't have to obsess about hair, I will not obsess about cancer either. I think you have bigger fish for me to fry, but help me to remember not to melt this wig, Lord! I don't want to be without it even for a day.

April 17, Saturday 12:59 PM

God has more than answered my prayers for a good wig. I've been smiling since Cheryl put it on me two days ago. I am so happy because I feel like myself, rather than me masquerading as someone else. Gone are Lucille Ball and Little Orphan Annie. Gone is the first wig which made me feel like an older woman just out from the beauty shop where they cut and teased each hair into plastic place. All I needed were gold sandals and bling to fit right in to some Florida retirement community. Now when I pass a mirror, Carolyn smiles back, the Carolyn who was in that looking glass four months ago before cancer and surgery and chemo altered my appearance–and my world.

The second test of the wig, after my visit to Ward's office, was yesterday when Andrew arrived home from college. He was unloading his car as I pulled into the driveway and stepped out of mine. A big smile filled his face, "Mom, you do look great–you look just like yourself! That wig is you!" His words were music to my happy ears!

And then, later in the day as Andrew and I shopped in the very same grocery store where a good friend had failed to recognize me a few days before, my new looks passed the ultimate test. As I stepped into the checkout line, the lady in front of me looked at me, smiled and said, "Hi, Weight Watchers®, right?"

"Yes, I'm Carolyn," I responded.

"Susan," she replied and we chatted as the checker checked

groceries. We had been in a start-up Weight Watchers® group together a few years previously, and she recognized me immediately. In fact, it was Susan who recognized me first. She was wearing her hair a darker shade than when we had last attended classes. It took a second look from me to realize I knew her, but she knew me immediately and initiated contact. I was so happy! Susan will never know what joy her greeting brought to my heart!

Our God is the God of the details. As I Peter 5:7 says, "Cast all your cares upon him, for he cares for you." God has graciously cared for this little corner of my life and I am grateful. I believe God also sent me a sweet little message recently. When Ward and I returned from the beach a week and half ago, we discovered a small bird's nest on our front porch, wedged between the bricks and the light sconce. Inside were five tiny little speckled eggs and we eagerly searched the internet to learn what kind of bird it might be. I could never see the bird well enough as she would fly from the nest, but based upon Ward's description I thought it might be a chickadee.

I really wanted to watch the babies hatch and grow as I had watched the previous year's brood who set up housekeeping in my door wreath. In that instance, I had taped paper over the inside glass in the door, punched pin holes in a couple of strategic places and watched within inches. Sometimes the mother bird and I would be eye to eye, separated by only two or three inches and the door glass. But that wouldn't work this year, so I consulted Andrew. "Is there some way I can hook up a camera to the porch and watch the bird nest on the computer?" By the time he got home yesterday, he had the problem solved. He brought home his computer camera, mounted in on the porch ceiling, trained it on the bird nest, and hooked it to Ward's laptop, perched on a small table inside the door. I can watch the mother sitting on her nest to my heart's content and she has no clue an admirer is two feet away.

Here is the big surprise for me: She is a sparrow, not a chickadee, not a wren like last year's clutch. She's just a simple, common, run of the mill sparrow. Nobody cherishes a sparrow. They are just an ordinary yard bird–not much different than two thousand years ago when Jesus said: "Are not two sparrows sold for a penny? Yet not one of them will fall to the ground apart from the will of your Father. And even the very hairs of your head are all numbered. So don't be afraid; you are worth more than many sparrows."[6]

Here's the bigger surprise. When I went to look up the above verse about the sparrow, I was shocked to discover that it is linked to the verse about the Lord God knowing the number of hairs on our head! In my mind, as I started searching for this verse I thought it was with the ones about God clothing the lilies of the field. No, it's about the hairs on my head, which are few in number now, but well camouflaged with my gorgeous wig! Furthermore, this passage reminds me how much my Heavenly Father cares for me. It reinforces the conviction that my life and times and passing are well known to him. He cares for the little sparrow, which has scant value to most of humanity. He cares for me. He cares about my hair! I am quite safe in my Father's hands.

Thank you, Father, for caring about my life and the hairs on my head! Thank you for sending your little sparrow to build her nest on my porch. Thank you that her presence sent me searching for the verse which surprised me with the reminder that you have numbered the hairs on my head. You bless me beyond what I could have imagined when I first saw her nest a dozen days ago. I thought that sparrow carried a general message from you, but it's a specific word tailored for me from you. Thank you so much, dear Father. Please watch over that little sparrow, bless her babies and shield them from predators, including mine and the neighbor's cats. I'll do my best to keep

---

6   Matthew 10:29-31

mine on house arrest. I know you made cats to hunt birds, but I'd appreciate it if you would initiate a peaceable kingdom on my front porch until these eggs can hatch and the little hatchlings fly safely away.[7]

April 20, Tuesday

Not More Cancer!

This is rich, really rich. My dog has cancer. I don't even know what lessons are to be learned here. She was fine but old, a few days ago, and then Sunday night when we returned from Blacksburg and visiting Dave, she did not come out from under the deck where her doghouse is until we coaxed and begged. It was very odd behavior for a dog who is usually barking to get in before we actually make it from the car door to the slider. Even odder, she would not take her evening medicine, which she considers a treat to be gobbled up. And she hadn't eaten the food left on the porch. Uncharacteristic for a beagle! They will eat anything! Yesterday, she continued lethargic and refused all food, drink and meds until late in the afternoon when she half-heartedly ate the pill on bread and a dog biscuit. This morning's vet visit confirmed my fears: Angel has cancer.

When I was in college, one of my English professors said that the most beautiful word in the English language is *murmur*. I don't know what the ugliest one is considered to be, but I vote for the word *cancer* to be high on that list–surely in the top ten. I'm not a dog person, but I do love my dog. This afternoon, I'll return to the vet with her and stroke her head gently as she dies. I cannot let this creature, who has been my constant companion for nearly 14 years, suffer through a disease which has no cure for her. For me, I hope and pray for a cure, but she is not so lucky.

---

[7]   *Author's note: Actually, she was a house wren. I don't know my birds, but God does!*

At least she will spend the afternoon asleep on her favorite spot, the sofa in the family room, blissfully unaware of her fate. She will just think she is going back to her hated vet hospital and then come home again. *Well, Lord, if there's a dog heaven, take good care of my beagle. God, who promised to see the sparrow fall, take notice of our little dog. God, who took note of the many cattle in Nineveh, bless her passing with peace and comfort. Who knew, at the front end of my journey, that I would walk through death with Angel our Beagle? You knew, God, you knew.*

April 21, Wednesday

Grieving

It is very quiet at my house this morning. No dog snores or begs for food or shakes her head to jangle her collar and tags for my attention. The cat alone is left to follow me from room to room and I wonder if she is curious about Angel's strange absence. The two of them were my sentries and shadows, but the cat follows silently on her stealth cat paws while the dog click-clacked her nails from room to room just in case the jangling collar was not enough to confirm her presence. Now it is a bit eerie with quiet and I'm glad for the raindrops to make at least some sound as my fingers touch the keyboard. I am still struck by the irony that my dog would die from cancer as I wage my own battle with the Big C foe. Angel was old in dog years, and I'm hoping I still have many people years to go; we shall see. God did honor my prayer for Angel: She passed swiftly in peace and comfort. *Thank you, God of man and beast.*

April 28, Wednesday

My Very Quiet House

The past week has been a hard one as I grieved Angel's death. I miss the many interactions we had throughout the day, her barking to go in and out the door, her companionship on walks–I don't think I know how to go for a walk with no dog on a leash. I miss the click-clack of her toenails on the floor, her jiggling collar tags, and the funny way she followed me from room to room. Even when I was cleaning, and moving back and forth between rooms, she would follow me with a quizzical look on her face that said "Mom, would you please settle somewhere? I don't know where to lie down." I miss the silly way she watched me when I got on the telephone. At those moments, she either tried to sneak up the steps (forbidden), or needed to go out, or needed fresh water or food. She was truly the toddler of the family. I now have to clean up every morsel of food which drops on the kitchen floor as I cook. I also have to sweep under the table when meals are done, because my doggie disposal unit is gone.

There are things about dog ownership I will not miss. No more poop patrol of the back yard, no more waking up in the wee morning hours because the dog needs to go out, and no more rushing home from errands because I fear I've overstayed her elderly bladder. We can slip away for the weekend without calling a dog sitter. The cat can survive a long weekend alone with a big bowl of water, another of food, and a clean litter box. If dogs are toddlers, cats are teens. They have the ability to totally ignore their "mom". They can also hear their owner's voice and yet make a different decision than what the master instructed. I frankly love their independent nature. Still, my cat follows me from room to room just like Angel did, and she is quick to sit on my lap if I sit down anywhere. She's a great companion, but she will not walk on a leash, and she is not very demanding of my time, except for lap space. Her low maintenance lifestyle is sharp contrast to the needy toddler who demanded so much of my time.

Still, in the days since I had Angel put down, I have also put down two containers of ice cream, one or two packages of cookies, some peanuts and potato chips and probably some other things I can't currently remember as I tried to swallow my sadness. I am confident that it was at least five pounds of food, because that's the amount the scale has risen since she died. At this rate, if I don't get control of my emotional eating, I'll have to buy new clothes for Andrew's graduation for the second time. Come to think of it, I am a great shopper. Ward says shopping is my spiritual gift. I pretty sure I have others, but I'm very good at exercising this one.

I am thankful that last week was filled with real estate details as we prepare to close on the townhouse: two home inspections, many calls and emails, a visit home from Andrew. It shortened the amount of time I had for tears. The tears took their toll, though, or more likely it was the chemo. I've lost about half the eyelashes I had. I didn't see them go, they dropped out silently, perhaps on the tissues, which blotted my eyes, perhaps from the allergies which caused me to rub my eyes too often, but most likely from the chemo, since that is a side effect. I still have enough lashes to plump up with mascara and I think I'll not try to remove it each night, or at least not most of it. My main eyelash consultant, Tracy my niece, suggested that I not try to use the false ones unless all lashes exit. She says sometimes the eyelash glue pulls out a few lashes, and I have no extra to spare. I've never had gorgeous eyelashes anyway, so I probably look more normal with thin real ones that full fake ones.

The real estate deal also presented additional blessings last week. On Wednesday, my Realtor, Lacy, and I spent about 2 ½ hours together at the townhouse while the inspector went over everything with a fine-tooth comb. Eventually, I told her I'm on chemo right now, and she shared her husband's story. He has just finished a grueling course of chemo treatment himself. So she understood some of what I've been going through. Then, she said the words that were music to my ears "You haven't lost your hair, have you?"

"Oh, yes I have," I replied, "This is a wig."

And she seemed genuinely surprised. She said she had no idea it was not my real hair.

My plastic surgeon was equally surprised when she came into the room to do my last expansion Monday. She said, "Usually, when I walk in the room, I see that the patient is wearing a wig and I think, 'chemo patient'. But when I looked at you, I thought it was your natural hair and didn't realize immediately that you are on chemo. You look so good!" I was greatly pleased!

Wednesday night, Lacy called me. "*USA Today* is doing an article on me about first time home buyers and they want to take pictures of me working with a client. Since you are the mom of a first time home buyer and will be doing the walk through with me tomorrow, would you mind if the reporter follows us around taking pictures?"

"Of course I'd be happy to do that!" I replied.

Lacy laughed, "Good, because I've already told him it would be fine. I didn't think you'd mind."

It was my turn to laugh. "You knew a ham when you saw one, Lacy."

We had fun the next day, and on Monday, our picture was front page of the Money section and also on page three. Ward's cousin was away on business in Illinois and was shocked to see a family member on the pages of a national newspaper. I've now had my fifteen minutes of national fame, I suppose.

Life goes on with cancer, and that's a good thing. I would hate for all of my life to be defined by cancer and its treatments. I like to look at this as just a phase I'm passing through. Although it has its limitations, I like to think of this as my well-earned sabbatical. It's my time for solitude, and thinking and writing. Professors get these kinds of breaks routinely. So Professor Mom gets her day–and weeks and months!

Monday night, Ward's mom called about eleven and said that Lou, Ward's dad, had collapsed while trying to walk to the bathroom, the third time that day. It was time for Nurse Carolyn to snap into action. Ward had also been called to help with the second collapse as he returned home from work earlier in the day. But this third event told me before we even got to the house that it was time for a hospital visit. I felt strongly that calling the rescue squad would be the best choice, considering his weakened state. I couldn't imagine a car ride buckled upright in a seat belt or trying to navigate a potentially packed waiting room of people with viruses and other infections.

My gift seems to be getting Lou to agree, even if reluctantly, to go to the hospital. It happened once before when we were in Hawaii and that time had possibly saved his life when a blood clot developed in his leg. This time, I suspected dehydration since he had experienced severe GI upset the day before. I was worried that his electrolytes might be out of whack as well. We called the rescue squad. He was admitted to the hospital. Thankfully the doctor said the next day that we had made the right choice. More thankfully, Lou is doing much better today and I am happy that they are considering home physical therapy to help build his strength back up. I know he'll feel better when he can do more. He's always been so involved in my sons' lives, as with all his grandchildren, and we are anxious to see him feeling more capable again. Life goes on, even with cancer, and I'm grateful to be part of the bigger family picture. For someone who only practiced nursing a few years, I did OK Monday night.

April 28, Wednesday

Surprise!

Last night was the biggest surprise party I have ever had—and by that I mean biggest as far as totally unexpected and unanticipated. Ward and the boys gave me a surprise birthday party for my fiftieth, and I was surprised by the beauty, size and detail of it, but I had some suspicions that something was up—I just didn't know what. It's hard to keep a total secret when you live with someone. But, my bunko group completely surprised me with an encouragement party "Celebrating Carolyn". It was so unexpected. My first hint was a sign on the front door, which said, "Celebrating Carolyn". I thought, "Oh, isn't that sweet," as I opened the door, expecting that to be the evening's surprise. But no, that was just the beginning. The next thing I noticed was that everyone wore pink, complete with pink sparkly leis. I was pinned with a pink corsage and given a lovely wine goblet with pink polka dots and my initial on it. Anne Kraft was the hostess and she had decorated in a pink theme, complete with pink cosmos, nonalcoholic so I could enjoy it, and finished with chocolate cupcakes topped with pale pink icing and pearl white sprinkles—so elegant! All the food was delicious, much of it served in pink dishes. A big sign bordered in pink said "We are so proud of you, Carolyn" and the ladies signed the edges with words of encouragement. I'll treasure it always. But more importantly, I'll treasure the loved wrapped up in that room poured out by a bunch of ladies who didn't even know me this time last year. God tucks blessings in the most unexpected places.

Today during my nurse practitioner check-up, I got more good news. I can enjoy fresh vegetables and fruits, including berries, as long as I wash them. On week three after treatment, I can enjoy the meat and fish I like cooked medium rare. That's a real treat for me, because I've grown weary of chicken and roast as my protein mainstays. She explained that the injection that rebuilds my immune system makes many of the older food advisories obsolete, mushrooms excepted. I'm happy to be able to expand my culinary experiences to meats that don't taste like shoe leather or fish that is dry and crumbly in my mouth. This might mean that I also don't have to be quite as rigid about what I can clean. Should I share this with Ward, or should I enjoy my housekeeping vacation? House cleaning has never been my cup of tea anyway. Decisions–decisions and ethical dilemmas! Of course I'll tell him–eventually I will, but really, it's a temptation! I still can't dig in dirt–flowerbeds, especially old mulch and leaves, must be avoided. Deep cleaning is not recommended –spores, viruses and germs are still a real threat, but week three sounds like a vacation compared to how I have been living to avoid hazards. My world has expanded greatly by this news.

Still, even as I look back on this sad week following Angel's demise, I am encouraged by the many blessings God tucked into it to give me distractions and comfort, encouragement and purpose. And blessings: rich, generous, grace-filled blessings. God's unmerited favor poured out upon me. *Thank you, Heavenly Father, for loving me with your limitless undeserved love. Thank you for causing my portion to fall in pleasant places. Life goes on and I'm thankful that you go right along with me!*

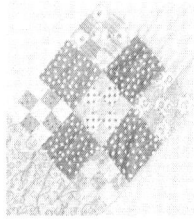

Chapter 5: MAY
Happy Distractions

May 26, Wednesday

Chemo, Round Four

Today I sit for my fourth chemo infusion and will find out in a little while if I will have additional treatments or if this is my last one. I have mixed emotions about that, since the first treatment plan was for four to six treatments. I don't know if I want six–additional insurance against recurrence–or if the difference between four and six is actually significant. I picked a doctor in whom I have great confidence, and beyond that, I trust God to direct her decisions for me and my particular needs. So, whatever her decision, I must practice having confidence both in her choices and more importantly in God's ability to direct her decisions, whether or not she is aware of his direction.

The third round was a bit more fatiguing, but it has still been a very easy course of treatment in my opinion. Taste buds are pretty well compromised and fatigue was a bit more of a companion this time around, but then again, I was putting more demands upon myself than I had after the first two treatments. The process of purchasing and furnishing a townhouse certainly placed more physical and mental demands upon my time, as did the emotional challenge of grieving for little Angel dog. Following my last treatment, we had to make an overnight trip to North Myrtle and a day trip to UVA the same weekend. The trip to UVA was a real joy to see Andrew inducted into Phi Beta Kappa, but following hard on the heels of the trek to the beach and back, I was really wiped out by Monday!

I did have a grumpy day or two this time around. Sometimes, I guess I'm just weary of being the good little chemo gal. I miss my other life, the one I had before cancer rudely invaded my carefully crafted plans. What a confirmation of the scripture, which says, "Man says, 'I will do this or that' ... but the Lord directs our days." In fact, he's always been in charge of my days; I just assumed I had more than I may actually have. It's a good thing that God does not let us see our future numbers of days or we might not accomplish all that he has planned for us. When we have a clearer sense that time might be limited, I suppose we are challenged to use the time more wisely. I am carrying a bucket list in my head, but not like the guys in the movie. My bucket list has little to do with places to go or adventures to pursue. It's more about leaving a legacy for those I love: picture albums carefully arranged and labeled, letters and notes, family history, scriptural lectures and lessons I have taught, and learned at the hand of my Lord. My immediate plans when I finish chemo are to get back my strength, get back into Weight Watchers® and get to the weight I want to be–and grow hair!

I want to work on this book, which is currently just loose journal pages and essays: collections of my thoughts along the way, as well as prayers and amazing interventions God has placed along my path. This past chemo session has been devoid of deep thoughts, and perhaps that has been the hallmark of much of my life. The Tyranny of the Urgent I believe one writer called it–the mundane, but urgent moments of life rush in demanding our attention, while the really important stuff of eternal consequences is easily pushed to the bottom of the list. I must be more careful to spend the majority of my moments on the important stuff of life.

May 28, Friday

God is the Best Sunscreen!

In the midst of a less than fun year, God continues to send me little presents of his presence. Andrew's graduation weekend was a blessing. Besides carrying the images of my precious first born son walking down the lawn at UVA in cap and gown, and later walking across a stage to actually receive his diploma in hand, I will remember the big tree on the UVA lawn. Who knew a big tree would figure so prominently in my graduation memories? For weeks I had planned how I would handle the baking May sun in Virginia. I had purchased a big sun hat to wear instead of a wig, thinking it would be a blistering day. I had searched out which side of the lawn would be shady for the longest period of time. I had a large purse in which to carry sunscreen and bottled water to stay hydrated. I was prepared.

Then, a few days before the big walk down the lawn, the weather reporters began to warn about showers, rain and even thunder storms for graduation day. So instead of the pre-planned sun protection, the morning of graduation I packed ponchos and umbrellas and an extra pair of older sandals in case the lawn was muddy. I packed small towels to wipe off wet chairs, and an extra towel and socks for a son I expected to be soaked following the outdoor event.

But it didn't actually rain that morning. It was cloudy, and the chairs were damp from the overnight monsoon, but that was quickly remedied. I was able to wear my wig instead of the giant sun hat, and we positioned ourselves on the shady side of the lawn in case the sun might come out later. And it did. About eleven o'clock, blue skies and sunshine broke through the cloud cover. We were near two tall ancient trees, and their round canopy overlapped to form a deep "V" shape, like a woman's V-neck dress, and the sun threatened to break above that V. I worried and watched as the sun rose in the sky, concerned that I'd get hot, or sunburned in my compromised chemo state. I slathered on sunscreen, and I watched. I need not have been worried; my heavenly Father directed his sun to rise in the sky in such a way that it followed the lollipop circle of the tree. Always, for the last hour of that ceremony, the sun was tucked just behind the tree's round profile, following that curve as it rose in the sky. I was always covered by the shade of that ancient tree's profile. I know that one with a more scientific mind would say that the sun just followed its orbit as the earth turned on its axis to cause it to rise on a curve. But I know my heavenly Father ordained that tree to grow in just that place for me that morning–the finger of God continuing to reach out to me and say, "I'm watching you. I've got everything under control." How many other men or women through the ages have enjoyed the shade of that great tree, unaware that it was put there for their joy and on this day for my protection. We serve an awesome God! I'll bet he's blessed many people with that very tree, and now, he has also blessed me.

God's blessings don't stop with a tall tree. In the midst of a time when I wonder if I look normal and I fuss with wigs and a hair-challenged head, God continues to send little messages of assurance to me that I look okay. Wednesday night, in my steroid-induced burst of energy following chemo, I was still cleaning and vacuuming the house about midnight. Andrew had a couple of friends over, with whom I had been chatting earlier in the evening. Finally, as they sat out on the porch, one of them said to him, "What is your mother doing cleaning this late at night?" Now in all truthfulness, in all the years these guys were in and out of my house when they were in high school, they never ever saw me cleaning at midnight. In fact, they more often probably saw me asleep on the couch at that hour! Now, after having been away at different universities, not all of my sons' friends know about my recent battle with the Big C. So Andrew explained my uncharacteristic cleaning frenzy. And his friends' response: "You are kidding! I had no idea! Your mom looks great, I can't believe she's on chemo!" And I love those precious young men for mistaking me for normal! Bless their hearts. I'm grateful to God for giving me energy and enthusiasm and drugs that haven't wreaked havoc on my body, mind or spirit.

Then yesterday, I got another sweet affirmation from the nurse who gave me my post-chemo injection. When she looked at my chart, she said, "I can't believe this is your correct age! I wouldn't have guessed you are over 49." She is now my favorite nurse in the Richmond area, and maybe even the world, because I turned 60 last November! But she didn't stop there. "Your wig looks great, too, so natural, you just don't look like someone on chemo." I'll love her forever. If I hadn't seen her there before, I might have suspected that God sent an angel to minister to me. In fact, he didn't need to send an angel; he simply inspired another of his children to offer me a blessing in audible terms. He speaks to my heart often; but yesterday, he spoke through the lips of a sweet nurse who took the time to send me out of her treatment room with an injection, words of affirmation, and a great big smile on my face. *Thank you, God, for the many ways you say, "I love you."*

May 31, Monday

Just Another Chemo Patient

I got caught up in a weird situation this past Saturday night. My hero of the evening was an ER physician valiantly trying to deliver excellent care to me after the on-call physician for my regular oncologist ordered me to any nearby ER for some lab work. My ordeal started after 24 hours of chills and sweats, with a slightly elevated fever. Before the night was over, I deeply regretted my decision to even call and report my symptoms. I know if I have a similar event again I will wait much longer to see if the condition subsides before I call for help. I hope that won't be a fatal mistake.

I suspected that it was going to be a long ordeal when I first talked to the on-call physician and learned that I would need to go to an emergency room for tests. After all the emphasis my care team had put upon calling if I had chills, even if no fever was present, I had decided this was the night to call. I had intermittent hours of chills since the previous night with periods of sweats. Nothing hurt out of the ordinary following chemo, but my experience with chills following chemo in the previous series had been much less concerning; a few chills on the Friday night following treatment, no sweats, no fever. This time seemed different. Oh, was it different!

I got to the ER and it was filled with folks hacking and coughing, apparently using the ER for their Saturday night doctor's office. I pleaded for a place to wait in isolation and a gracious triage nurse accommodated me–I was shuffled off, with mask, to an unused treatment room with some dilapidated-looking equipment in it, but I was grateful that the only other human there was my husband. We quickly closed the adjoining door where a triage nurse evaluated a coughing preschooler. I had images of giant germs lunging at me from every quarter. I felt doomed.

Within a few minutes I was moved to the ER where a flimsy curtain separated me from the next patient who appeared to be a mother with a husband and young children in tow. Once again, I heard coughing, and could see little tennis shoes beneath the curtain. I envisioned more germ monsters seeping into my space.

The ER nurse was efficient at drawing my blood for a CBC and culture–and very good. She got both veins the first time, a near miracle for me because I have tiny, deep, rolling veins. Then we waited, and waited, and waited…for hours.

The ER doctor, who would become my hero before the night was over, popped into my space to explain that he was waiting for my on-call oncologist to return his call and direct his next steps in my care. My CBC came back with elevated white counts, a sign of infection, but so far, no infection site was evident. Urinalysis was a little suspicious, but not indicative of a significant infection, chest X-ray was clear, no pain, and no outward signs of infection or inflammation. The ER physician was incredibly compassionate towards me and in the course of the evening I learned that he had gotten to know chemo up close and personal as his teenage daughter battled cancer. He was concerned that a seemingly slight sign of infection in an immunocompromised person like myself could be dangerous, even lethal. I appreciated his medical knowledge and even more his heart for a chemo patient on the opposite end of the age spectrum from his precious daughter. He had been through this sort of fever spike with her on three occasions and no infection site was ever found, and he was unwilling to leave any stone unturned for me, either. He was the epitome of what I envision physicians should be and I was incredibly grateful that my name landed on his case list that night.

In the course of the evening, as we watched the hands of the clock march round and round its face, my ER doctor would periodically come back to report that he was still unable to reach the on-call physician. Sometime after 11 PM, the chills and fever broke and I began to feel more normal. Still, we waited in our cubicle as the mother with children left and an elderly lady took her spot. I had heard what sounded like vomiting when she was out in the hallway, and now, through the curtain, I could hear her moan as she breathed heavily. I learned from the voices on the other side of the curtain that she was 82, had only one nephew in the area, and was a patient at a local nursing home. Her records weren't readily available but someone determined that she had no advanced directives.

Then we heard the urgent voice of the nurse attending her. "Need some help in here! She's not breathing!"

"Bag her, help her breath" a male voice responded.

"She's coding!"

"Bag her, bag her!"

There was a big flurry of activity on the other side of the curtain and I began to pray for the unseen lady there. She responded and there was momentary calm. They gave her oxygen, I think, and kept a close eye on her. I heard a female voice sweetly call her "Pumpkin" and explain kindly that they were doing these things that made her moan so they could help her. But later in the night, when her blood gases still weren't good, they intubated her. I breathed a sigh of relief at her chance to pull through this long night. I hope she makes it and her bed sores heal. I hope she has more sweet days with her nephew, and I hope she knows Jesus.

About 2:30 AM, I decided I'd had enough of waiting in an ER on a hard small metal bed. I got up carefully and moved into the corner where the curtains met, sheltered from the watchful eye of the security camera trained on my cement-like gurney. I put my street clothes back on and went to the nursing station to tell my ER physician I was feeling better and would go on back home now. He begged me not to leave, emphasized the danger to me as an immunosuppressed patient, and said he had contacted the hospitalist to see me. I would probably be admitted for a couple of days of antibiotic therapy. So I relented and returned to my curtained cubicle. He probably sent a desperation call to the hospitalist who appeared within moments and assured me I could send Ward home because I would be admitted. I wanted Ward to get some rest. He had travelled to North Carolina early Saturday morning to help his parents empty out the country house, his mother's home place which had recently been rented. Furthermore, he had to return his brother's large van by 8:00 AM Sunday morning, and it was now almost 3:00 AM. He needed rest.

When the hospitalist learned that the ER physician had been unable to reach the on-call oncologist, he asked my permission to consult with his hospital's oncologist, and I agreed. Their policy was to admit chemo patients in my circumstances. But the hospitalist decided to place one more phone call to the on-call doc. Finally, the on-call oncologist answered the phone. He ordered me home on a course of heavy-duty antibiotics. I called Ward. He had been asleep about ten minutes. As the ER doctor came to prepare me to return home, he told me the story of his teenage daughter. She is an athlete who has set state records in her sport and has now come to the attention of an Olympic medalist and coach. She also has become a motivational speaker for others walking the oncology route. This young athlete's ordeal has transformed into an opportunity for blessing, and that night, her dad blessed me.

The hospitalist made me promise to call my oncologist first thing Monday morning and I did promise. Of course, that call will not happen now until Tuesday, because this Monday is Memorial Day. My own oncologist will not be available this long holiday weekend and I don't want to try to deal with any other on call doctors who don't know me except as the patient of their colleague. Saturday night had been way too complicated for me to want to go for round two.

I did not have a great time in the ER that weekend, but I will always be grateful for the ER physician who reached out to me with kindness, excellent care, and a desire to protect me even from myself when I had reached the end of my patience. Thank you, Doctor, for standing in the gap for me Saturday night. I pray your daughter has a full recovery and a long and productive life. I hope she breaks Olympic records as she serves as an inspiration for people everywhere who do battle with cancer. May she have a life of joy and happiness and be blessed with a husband and children if that's what she wants. And may my Lord God repay you richly for your kindnesses to me on Saturday night. I'm living on the short end of my life, but I pray that your precious daughter's life has just begun.

Chapter 6: JUNE
Chemo Gets Tiresome

June 2, Wednesday

Job, the OT Sufferer

I've thought about Job a lot these past few days, not because I
think my challenges are similar to his, they are not. My trials
beside this Old Testament saint's trials are easy and light. I
think of the Apostle Paul's words in 2 Cor. 4:17: "For our light
and momentary troubles are achieving for us an eternal glory
that far outweighs them all." I see my cancer as a temporary
bump in the road; even so, I am aware that I may be on the
first installment of a long and challenging journey. Yet I'm not
thinking about Job on my behalf today. I'm thinking of Job
because I had a precious hour or so Saturday afternoon with a
friend whom I have not seen for many years. Still, we are sisters
of the heart and we have shared email prayer requests, sporadic
news blips and annual Christmas updates. Ester[1] and I met
when she was a student at a local university. I ran a rooming
house where she rented a room from me. She was, and still is,
one of the most upbeat Christian women I have ever known.
She nurtured me in the faith when we lived together. She had
been a Christian for a long time and I was new to the faith. I
will never forget the many sweet times we spent in fellowship
with one another and with Jesus.

---

1   *Not her real name*

But Ester has three adult children none of whom currently walk with the Lord. One apparently has deep and severe mental, emotional and/or spiritual issues. She has isolated herself from family, friends and her past. I am heartbroken for Ester and have spent the past days with this troubled child nestled against my heart. I want the happy ending for Ester. I want her prodigal daughter to come to her senses and return to the home where she is loved and treasured. I want her to see the unconditional love which her mother holds for her; the acceptance and healing which await her. Life took some hard turns for this child/woman, and she's trying to recreate herself in some unrecognizable form. When circumstances in life whirled beyond her control, she despised herself for being unable to prevent harm to herself, and now she's determined to create her own forms of self-destruction. She's trying to divorce herself from love (and I suspect feelings) in all its forms: parental, Godly, friendship, love for self or others. How deep must be her hurt and pain! As Ester told the pieces of the story she knows or speculates about, her eyes filled with tears. So did my heart.

It doesn't seem fair, Lord, that one who loves you must suffer such loss. I envision Ester as a young mother, offering lessons in Christian faith to her young children. They should have blossomed into adults of faith, even as I did under Ester's tutelage. I guess I want a magic formula: if you raise your kids this way, they will turn out thus. But raising kids, like all of life, is not a predictable recipe with a guaranteed result. I suppose you know that better than most, Heavenly Father! There are few Cinderella stories, even in the world of faith. Otherwise, everyone would rush to the ball wearing glass slippers. Instead, we are born into a crumpled world. We hobble into adulthood and bear our own children in hope and great expectation. We raise them as best we can, knowing that you have created each individual with the freedom to choose.

So my prayer for Ester's daughter is this: Lord God, protect her from herself. Banish the darkness that blinds her. I know we see

only moments in time, but you see the big picture. Please, Lord
God, deliver her from the mental and spiritual prison which
binds her. Compel her to seek help where your love is ministered.
Forgive me for calling you unfair, Lord God. I know we live in a
fractured world. But you have the power to fix the brokenness, in
any form. Please, God, set her spirit and her mind free. You alone
are up to this challenge.

I pray this prayer knowing that you are able, Lord, yet aware that
we live in a hurting world, where children sometimes do not come
home. Relationships are not mended. Healing does not come on
this side of heaven. Hearts break. Families crumble along with the
dreams they once held hopefully. Pain and sickness and broken
parts are not reserved exclusively for the ones we think deserving
of such fate. We all have our times of suffering, disappointment,
and challenges beyond comprehension. Our sense of fairness
is not like yours, Lord God. Nor is our timing yours either.
Sometimes we walk wounded through a distressed world, trusting
you to make sense for us of the seemingly senseless events which
confront us. Each of us is a little Job sometimes, bearing burdens
which we do not understand.

You restored Job's lost wealth and gave him more sons and
daughters. But the first ones who died in his time of trial were
still gone. Yet Job trusted you, Lord God, even when his wife
urged him to curse you and die. He trusted you. His heart no
doubt had a hole in it where his deceased sons and daughters'
memories dwelt, but he trusted you. As he sat among his restored
and multiplied blessings, I know he still carried a tender spot for
the children who could not share his latter day blessings. But he
trusted you. Grant us strength to trust you, Lord, even on the
hard roads of confusion and suffering.

June 3, Thursday

Boring is Good

My oncologist called yesterday afternoon with words that made my heart soar.

"Carolyn, I'm looking at the most boring labs on you!"

"Great! Boring is good." I replied.

I learned from her that the chills and elevated white count were most likely from the blood cell booster injection I'd received on Thursday. Even if I had contracted a little something, she explained, my blood counts were so good that I had fought it off with my own reserves. I could stop the dreaded antibiotic, which caused me to wake Ward up screaming the previous night. I slept on the couch last night since I'd already taken my daily dose before my wonderful oncologist called. I didn't want my nightmares to awaken him again. Thankfully, I slept with peace and calm, the answer to my prayer before I fell asleep.

In most of life, I hope I am an interesting person. But to my oncologist, I'd love to be a boring, run-of-the-mill patient who follows the ideal textbook course, has a cure, and never has to challenge her creative medical juices again. Boring is great in medicine; I don't want to be the woman remembered for her valiant, losing battle with cancer. The first time I understood boring in the medical field was one day when I did a clinical rotation in labor and delivery during my days as a student nurse. The staff nurse said, "Usually, labor and delivery is pretty routine. You do the same thing day in and day out. But when it's interesting or dramatic, it is almost never good. That means something has gone terribly wrong, and nobody wants that." I don't want that either! So *just keep me boring, Lord, just keep me boring.*

Telephone Solicitations

I hate telephone solicitations. I'm on every do not call list I know about. I have little patience with those who call anyway. I hate political phone calls, too, but unfortunately, the legal fat cats who swell our government with self-protection, kept those calls legal, along with solicitations from non-profits. I do not take kindly to these calls, either, even if they are legally within their rights to interrupt my day to try to guilt me into giving to their cause.

So why is this on my mind today? Because now the calls have started from every cancer and breast cancer fundraising network know to woman. "Mrs. Mustian, this is so and so with the breast cancer whatever organization." It does not endear these people to me that they think because I have been victimized by a disease I am happy to now be fair game to their efforts to prey on my misfortune. I hate telephone solicitations and I do not appreciate telephone reminders that I have recently gotten to know breast cancer up close and personal. If I should somehow forget that fact, I'm sure I'll quickly remember when I disrobe for my next shower. So please, if you are a telephone solicitor for some fund raising cause, know that I will not talk to you and never, ever donate for any cause for any reason over the phone. Mail me information if you want, but do not interrupt my busy life or peaceful rest period to beg money. I am not a boring person when it comes to telephone solicitations–I'm a grizzly bear, and a mad one at that! I want to be remembered as the woman you never want to call again!

And one more thing, while I'm on my soapbox. If you work for one of these organizations or volunteer with them, God bless you. I know you are working to raise money for the cure and doing many good things for people who need the emotional and physical support to deal with the devastation this illness can create. I know that research dollars buy medical brains and energy to spend hours and days and years in labs looking for

a breakthrough. I know that. And I am grateful, truly I am.
In fact, I'm participating in a research study as I go through
chemo. But do not dial my phone number and interrupt the
sanctity of my home with your sales pitch, no matter what
you are pitching. Thank you. I'm going back to sewing Roman
shades for my son's new place and I hope I am not interrupted
needlessly again.

Caregivers and Needy Folks

This little incident reminded me of another encounter I
had with one of the help groups about the time I started
chemo. They offered a free service which some friends had
encouraged me to try. Ward went with me, just for fun.
Before the service was delivered, they had each of us fill
out paperwork and he was asked his relationship to me. He
marked Spouse. The woman going over his paper said, "Are
you also her care giver?"

"NO!" I said emphatically. "I take care of myself! He's my
husband."

"Well, he gives you emotional support, doesn't he?"

"Yes, he's wonderful. But he's not my caregiver. I don't need
taking care of. I take care of myself."

"Well, I'm going to just mark caregiver on here, too. I'm sure
he's a caregiver."

I wish I had just gotten up and walked out at that moment.
Perhaps I would have gotten my point across. But I didn't.
I desperately wanted the service they offered. But it was a
degrading experience to feel I had been reduced to a pitiful,
helpless sick person. In retrospect I felt that because of cancer,
I had also lost my dignity and value in that woman's eyes. It
seemed to me she only saw me as someone to be taken care
of. I felt like my condition justified her agency's existence. It
seemed to me that I had simply become another check box on
a form, just a number on a report of services delivered.

Now I'm hesitant to go for free services. I fear that "free" services carry a high cost. They place the participant in a dependent, needy posture, and I don't do well in that role. Maybe one day I'll be in such a state, in hospice or in a nursing home. I hope even there I'll be treated as a whole human, worthy of dignity and respect, and not pity. However, I know the chances of that are slim. But for today, I am a very capable woman, busy living life fully, even in the midst of a series of chemo treatments which temporarily curtail some of my more social activities. I am a very capable woman with a mostly bald head who must be careful of potential infections. But I'm certainly not lying around being cared for and tiptoed around like some fragile, helpless houseplant. I take care of myself, thank you very much!

June 4, Friday

Impatience, Anger and Other Unattractive Things

This must be my week for impatience with the world. I suppose as a psych nurse I would say I am in the angry phase of the grief process (thinking of grief in the broad sense of any loss or disappointment). But honestly, I've always been annoyed with incompetence and I don't have to be grieving anything to be irritated with poor service–or poor judgment for that matter!

One week and one day ago, we switched from DSL to a cable internet service to improve speed, reliability and coverage throughout our house. Today, about noon, my internet inexplicably stopped working. I went to the "fix-it-yourself" program the technician installed on my computer and started working through the instructions step by step. Then I got to the part that described about eight steps of opening the unit with a screw driver, plugging and unplugging various devices, and removing and reinserting a battery in the backup unit. Problem was, the technician had installed all of that equipment in the crawl space under my house. Bigger problem: chemo patients can't be crawling around in dirt, dust, moisture and who knows what germs under the crawl space of a house! I knew the technician had installed stuff under there, but he told me it would only require a battery change every couple of years. This was day eight, a good 720 days earlier than I expected to have to deal with the wet, dirty underbelly of the house!

I got angry. How many home owners routinely crawl under their house to repair computer service equipment? What if I have to go on chemo again in a year or two? I called the company. I was not a sweet little old lady. I told them it is impossible for a chemo patient to be expected to crawl under their house to mess with the multiple units installed under there and they would need to move the equipment inside my house if I'm expected to work on it. They told me there might be a charge for this visit and I told them I did not expect to pay anything. They would not guarantee there would be no charge and I would not agree to any charge. I asked for a supervisor–none were available. I've learned they never are available, but I continue to ask. I asked for a technician today. They said none were available: Sunday would be the earliest service call. Today is Friday, two days away from Sunday. Then the man on the other end of the phone called the Richmond repair center and managed to get a technician for tomorrow. I was happy with that.

Maybe 30 minutes later, a nice technician called and said he could be on his way to my house within minutes. I was delighted. He came, he fixed the internet, and he moved the system into my furnace room where all the other household equipment is, like the furnace obviously, the hot water tank, and the main switch to the household current. He was very efficient, done in less than an hour. Turns out, the unit had been draining the battery backup, because he said the outlet under the house was faulty. I did notice when he had first opened the door that the light bulb which was previously there was missing and an electrical plug outlet with a naked socket at the end had been installed by the previous tech. Who knows what dirt, bugs or moisture had entered that open socket.

As he was getting ready to leave, I thanked him and asked him to be sure the ticket for tomorrow gets pulled so someone doesn't show up for a repair already completed. I told him I was quite surprised to get service this afternoon. He explained that they try to get to medical emergencies immediately–those tickets are moved to the front of the line. I was shocked. I didn't think of myself as a medical emergency. I thought of myself as a homeowner with a particular medical inability to service my own computer/telephone/cable equipment. I felt badly about being moved to the front of the list. I'm not in an emergency, just temporarily restrained from my normal activities, including messing around in dirt and grime. Can one be in a medical emergency when one is without communication equipment that did not exist just a few years ago? I suppose so, but still, I didn't mean to present myself as an emergency. I did mean to communicate my frustration with an impossible situation, and I must have done that quite effectively. I was angry about being inconvenienced because someone didn't think about the implications of putting equipment in an awkward space. Does the company train employees in such things? But I am grateful, very grateful, to have my internet back! And I'm very appreciative to have had a young man willing to spend the few extra minutes to move the equipment to a location that makes sense for me and for future techs who might need to access it.

Even if I hadn't been on chemo, I'm not sure that equipment, which a homeowner is expected to access, should be positioned in such an awkward place. What if it's nighttime, or winter, or muddy and rainy or snowy? What if, as I age, I get less agile? What if snakes or creepy bugs get on me while I'm under there? Will I live to get out? I don't mean because of them killing me; I mean because I may have a heart attack and die of fright as I scramble to try to get away. I wish I had a clearer understanding of how I would need to be involved with this equipment before the first tech installed it there last week–I wouldn't have agreed to it then, and I could have avoided all this hassle today. But then again, that would have required a thoughtful, carefully informed decision and I wasn't given the information to make that decision. I did get about a dozen reminder phone calls, text messages and email communications reminding me of the initial installation appointment last week. Perhaps they should have used one or two of those communications to convey some useful information, because surely after the first half dozen, I was saturated with their annoying reminders.

I wish companies would think beyond the end of their noses; they'd have happier customers and maybe less people would be losing jobs today. Just maybe … well, that's what I'm talking about. I get impatient with individuals and corporations that just think of the quickest way to turn a buck without thought for the longer-term impact. Come to think of it, maybe they think they will get an extra service charge out of me because of this…think again. I also don't take kindly to being mistaken for a fool. I hope I communicated that clearly in my phone call when I reported the service need in the first place. Now that I've unloaded my frustration on technicians and internet systems and corporate American, I think I'll go spend a little down time enjoying the comforts and luxuries that corporate America has developed for us.

June 5, Saturday

Lookin' Good!

I woke up early this morning, a little before six, and turned on my small bedside TV with earphones to try to put myself back to sleep without waking up Ward. Alas, about fifteen minutes into the news cast, I heard the local announcer say, "If you're looking for the best yard sales in town today there's a big multi-family sale with NASCAR memorabilia, a couple of dirt bikes …" The announcer gave the intersection of my street. Now I'm not a NASCAR fan, but I do have yard sale blood running through my veins, although I rarely go to them anymore. Back in the day, when I was a financially challenged nursing student, one of my forms of entertainment was to take five dollars and go yard sale hunting on a Saturday morning. It was like a treasure hunt and I pretty much decorated my apartment with great finds. You could buy a lot of stuff for five dollars back then.

So I quietly slipped out of bed and went into the bathroom where I painstaking applied makeup and fixed my wig just right. I never leave the house without looking as good as I possibly can. I don't want anyone looking at me with that pitiful look: "Oh, that poor woman, she's on chemo." Therefore I usually avoid hats and scarves and opt for my wig instead.

This morning, when I was confident that my face and "hair" were well done, I quietly slipped back into the semi-dark bedroom where my husband slept. I put on the clothes I had left folded on the chair the night before, and carefully slipped my feet into the sandals I had left there beside the chair. Then I headed out the door, confident that I looked great. Most of my neighbors don't know about my chemo condition and I don't want my looks to telegraph that information. Not that it's a secret; it's just that I want them to know because I told them, and not because I look sickly.

I stopped at a neighbor's house and chatted for a few moments, giving her the good news that the yard sale made the local news. Her husband and daughter were busy carrying out sale items, so I didn't linger long. Then I moseyed on down to the house at the end of the street where Susie was also was busy displaying merchandise. The sale didn't technically start for an hour, but a couple of cars had already crept up the street as more neighbors brought out their castoffs.

Just as I stepped onto Susie's driveway, I looked down at my feet, which at the moment have a little chronic numbness because of the chemo I am on. Oh, my! On the right foot was my black sandal with four black cloth straps. And on my left foot: the two-strapped brown leather sandal with little flowers tooled into the design. So much for looking great! I looked like the crazy lady of the neighborhood who just wasn't quite right! I don't know why I strive so hard to look "normal"; normal hasn't been my forte for any of my life, so why should this year be any different!

I greeted Susie, pointed out my shoe drama, and we both had a good laugh. We chatted for a few moments and Susie told me that this yard sale was to sell things that belonged to her bachelor brother who died suddenly in January. He was only 45. We talked about grief and I empathized with her, sharing a little of my experience in dealing with grief when my sister died at age 39. I also told her about my recent bout with cancer. She actually has two friends on a similar path right now. She understood exactly what I am experiencing. She asked if we could get together sometime and I of course welcome the opportunity. I'll follow up with her on that soon.

I headed back toward home, stopping again at the first neighbor's house to laugh with her about my choice of shoes. She said I got A for effort in trying to be considerate of my sleeping husband. "Besides," she said, "I just consider such things the challenge of early mornings. Look at me, I'm wearing my regular glasses to see, and my sun glasses as a headband because I couldn't find one this morning!"

Women. You gotta love women! For all the stories about us being hard on each other, my experience has been mostly that we are encouragers and nurtures and spreaders of grace and mercy. We mostly know we are all doing the best we can in challenging times, even if the challenge is to pick out matching shoes in a dark bedroom!

I thought I was heading down the block this morning to give my neighbors a heads-up that they might expect heavy traffic today because of the news story. I also thought that I might find an item or two for Andrew's new townhouse. I was wrong. I was walking down that one-block long street to be a blessing to my neighbors and to receive blessings from them as well. I was walking down that street to have a couple of good laughs, share a few tears with a grieving neighbor, and to be reminded not to take myself too seriously on the "lookin' good" frontier. I should not have needed that reminder–who am I kidding! God's word tells us that our beauty and adornment should be that of a sweet spirit and the love of Jesus.[2] I must remember that lesson when my wig is making me sweat and my make-up is mostly rubbed off from dabbing at the perspiration, which runs down my face and neck on the hot summer days when a wig feels like wearing a stocking cap in 95-degree weather! *And Lord, thank you for my sweet neighbors so ready to minister laughter and caring and grace.*

---

2   *I Peter 3:3-4*

June 7, Monday

Drama Outside my Window

Yesterday and again this morning, I have spent some time watching the drama which unfolds daily just outside my window at the back of the house. Several years ago, we built two small ponds connected by a short ambling creek. We have a few koi in the bottom pond and of course I've planted flowers and shrubs around it over the years. A canopy of trees covers it, so grass doesn't grow well there, but it is cool and peaceful during the weekdays when the neighbors are all away, and I've come to think of it as my private sanctuary. I also placed three bird feeders out there and have invested a small fortune trying to find some that would be squirrel proof. What I've learned so far is that there is no such thing, in spite of what the packaging and promo materials might claim. Thus, the drama.

When I recently refilled the bird feeders, I heavily greased the poles with petroleum jelly to give the squirrels a bit of a challenge on their way to robbing my feeders. They can empty a large feeder in about a day, and our neighborhood is overrun by squirrels. I counted ten nests one spring, just in sight of my backyard. Of course these feeders are low to the ground and close to the fence and trees. It's an easy thing for squirrels to just jump on the feeder, but since it is on a foot-long wire, it swings and turns wildly and the squirrels don't seem to like that ride too much. Still, it makes for entertaining amusement for a woman who has probably been isolated a bit too long!

So here's the drama yesterday. The squirrels occasionally managed to knock a few seeds onto the ground then scramble to collect them. But the chipmunks are also scurrying back and forth along the fence and on the ground, hoping to be recipients' of the squirrels' efforts. When the little chipmunks get too close to what the squirrels have identified as their territory, quarrelling and chasing ensue. Sometimes, then, a bird will slip in and get a few seeds while the other animals are distracted. Sometimes the bigger birds cause the smaller ones to hold back, patiently awaiting their opportunity to feed. I do have a thistle feeder which I believe only the smaller ones can enjoy, so I hope everyone gets a turn at some table, but my best efforts still can't guarantee equity for everyone who hungers.

And one can't even tell who is really hungry and who is eating or gathering out of habit and opportunity. I've been guilty of that myself. Last fall, I heard that canned pumpkin was going to be in short supply. Now I don't use a lot of canned pumpkin, but I do use some, especially when I am actively working my favorite weight loss program. Pumpkin is a good low calorie substitute for oils and fats in many recipes. Just to be on the safe side, I purchased about a half dozen cans when I found some prominently displayed in the grocery store a few months ago. The canned pumpkin shortage is now here, and I still have six cans of pumpkin on my shelves. I don't know when I'll run into another recipe that calls for pumpkin, but in case it calls for six cans, I am ready! Maybe I'm a squirrel at heart, in woman skin! I do know I squirreled away six cans of pumpkin which I obviously haven't needed these past several months!

This morning, I watched another surprising drama. A huge black bird, a crow, I suppose because it was much larger than a starling, came into the outdoor sanctuary, closely followed by a scolding blue jay. Although greatly outsized by the black bird, that blue jay was determined that the crow would have no peace in my little garden and he harassed that big bird until it flew away. Now the black bird has returned with reinforcements–another crow, and the blue jay is systematically squawking and dive-bombing those big birds–and I think the blue jay is winning!

When I watch this little microcosm of our world, I am again reminded of man's futile attempts to grab and possess and control power and territory and supplies on this earth. It is an innate part of our broken world and cannot be resolved by war or peace conference or treaties or political power houses. No matter how much food or resources are available, there will be inequity of distribution based upon who has the most power or ability to control the source of supply. America sends ships of grain to hungry countries where it rots on docks or in warehouses or is hoarded by warlords who starve out the people groups out of favor with the ruling class. Corrupt leaders turned despots line their pockets with money diverted from the sufferers those funds were intended to serve.

Dr. Leslie Weatherhead,[3] a gifted theologian from early last century, expressed it much more eloquently than I ever could:

> God has provided enough for all his children. It is commonplace that the harvest never fails over wide areas at once. If there is famine in one place, there is plenty in another. Given the good will of the community, there is no reason on God's side why every man and woman in the world should not have enough to eat and enough to wear. But God depends on men to act as brothers, in order that his providence may be mediated. Life is a family affair. And it is treachery to the family spirit, and hostility to God, if the selfishness of some deprives others of their share of God's gifts. Man's free will is a terrible possession, for it means that by greed and selfishness he can to some extent, and sometimes does, defeat temporarily the purposes of a loving God.

I see Dr. Weatherhead's words played out in the little animal world outside my window. I look out on the mini world I created and see that my best efforts to provide food for the birds are thwarted by the bigger squirrels which hoard their food. I'll bet there are squirrel nests in these trees with bird seeds filled to the

---

3   Weatherhead, Leslie D. **A Shepherd Remembers**. *Abingdon-Cokesbury Press, New York, 1938. pg. 38.*

opening! I've thought about putting out squirrel/critter food, but I don't know if that would bring even more of them into the space, and it's only about 25 'X 40'; how many squirrels I can accommodate! Even among birds, they fight among kinds–just like we humans do. And I suppose they have their reasons: need to provide food and protection for their young, fear, inbred hatred for those unlike themselves. I don't know what goes on in the minds of birds, and I sure don't know what goes on in the minds of other humans. I am struck by how our Father's heart must break when he provides for his own and his own receive him not.

Oh, heavenly Father, what a challenge it must be for you to stay seated on your throne until your time is fulfilled. There must be days when you look down on this broken world and want to end this strife and greed and pain and suffering. But you wait patiently, until all whom you have called to you have answered your call. Thank you, God, that you wait patiently, not wanting any to be lost, but all to come to Jesus. Help me to be faithful to speak words of hope and life through Jesus Christ. Amen. And God, help me figure out how to make this yard a place where every little critter can get the food it needs. Thank you.

June 8, Tuesday

I Did Not See This Coming

I did not see this one coming. I suppose one never does. I went to my general surgeon yesterday for my first routine follow-up after the mastectomy. He found a troubling spot under my arm, which he initially decided was nothing. But he had lingered, questioning look on his face, just a little too long for me. "How confident are you that the place under my arm is nothing?" I asked as he was bringing the exam to a close. Neither of my past cancers raised concern with my doctors. The melanoma was so atypical in presentation that neither my internist nor my dermatologist thought it would be anything. Fortunately, my dermatologist had biopsied it, probably mostly for my own peace of mind. She may have saved my life. The nurse practitioner who initially examined my breast had also felt nothing and was also confident there was nothing there. She ordered the diagnostic x-ray as a precaution.

"Well," responded my surgeon, "let me just do an ultrasound on it." There was a large dark circle on the screen. "Probably a seroma" he said, and the nurse prepared a needle to drain it. It shrunk some as a teaspoon or two of fluid filled the syringe. But it didn't disappear as a seroma should have. I thought about my first radiologist telling me how frightened women are who have a lumpectomy and then have to return for mammograms every few months the first couple of years. "They come in shaking, nervous, fearful," she had said. I chose a double mastectomy partly to not have to fear possible recurrence. But there is breast tissue under armpits and simple mastectomies don't get that tissue. I was shaking, quaking on the inside.

"Can that fluid be biopsied?" I asked.

"I'm going to biopsy it," he responded, and I was relieved. I think he was avoiding the word "mass." He was quick and efficient with the procedure and assured me we would have results in two to three days.

"I don't know what this is," he said, "but it could be scar tissue, it could be necrotic fat." Fat would be nice, I thought. Fat is a lot nicer than a cancerous mass.

I have had a lot of surgery under that arm in the last few years; three plastic procedures to remove a benign cyst (the first two failed) and then the lymph node removal during the mastectomy. There's a lot of opportunity for scar tissue and I am hopeful that it will be something simple like that. But I can't help but think of my Aunt Lois who's first breast cancer returned about the time she finished chemo. I haven't even made it to the end of this first series of six treatments and I am hoping that this is also my only chemo ever required. But I must remember that life is uncertain in a broken world. I serve a risen Savior who guarantees my eternal health and healing, but not necessarily on this side of heaven. *Lord, keep me in perfect peace as I set my mind and heart upon you.*

Still, in this broken world, I have something to celebrate today. Ward and I have been married 25 years. We're going to eat out at a cheap restaurant tonight, because I'm holding out for the elegant one on Thursday when I will be free to choose whatever I want from the menu including medium rare steak if I want it! On Wednesday I start week three following chemo and that means freedom to choose tasty food! In an unpredictable world, Ward is my mainstay, my rock, my anchor. He will walk the hard journey with me, if that's my call. For today, one of my gifts to him will be a clean house! That will be a big surprise! Happy Anniversary, Ward. I love you. You are one in six-plus billion.

This afternoon I went shopping for an anniversary card. I had planned to get it yesterday, but following the biopsy, I needed to come home and put ice on the wound. I also figured a few hours of rest would be wise since we were going to Andrew's for the evening to finish hanging window treatments–well, at this point, Ward and Andrew were going to hang and I was going to supervise. At any rate, I began reading cards in the local card shop; lots and lots of cards. One card had a beautiful verse which ended with these words: "All I want is to grow old with you…to watch our life unfold and our dreams come true, one by one." It spoke of hoping for many more years and I didn't know if I even had months. I cried. I wondered if I was buying Ward our last anniversary card.

I don't know if I have time to grow old with Ward. I don't know if my dreams with him are done. I searched for a different card. None fit. I bought the one that made me cry.

At home, I chose a felt-tip pen to sign the bittersweet card. I penned my name real big as though the bold writing would ward off bad result and signify the brave hope I dared to hope–many more years to dream and live out those dreams with my prince of a husband. At that moment, I realized all my dreams have come true as Ward's wife. We have had a wonderful, blessed life, rich and full beyond measure. We have two great sons. We share faith in Christ. We still like each other after 25 years, not many couples can say that in this day and age. My dreams have come true, and I hope we have time to dream more dreams. But if not, I've lived a wonderful life beside my husband who was a gift from God beyond all I could have ever hoped or dreamed. *Thank you, God, that you have blessed me with a life which brings me joy and contentment as I look back over the years you have given us. I will be grateful if we have more years together, but I am also grateful for the many years you have given us. Your grace has been abundant in our lives.*

June 9, Wednesday

Rollercoaster Rides

"It's a rollercoaster ride, isn't it, Mom?" My son Andrew was responding to my great sigh of relief as I hung up my cell phone following a short conversation with my general surgeon. He called to tell me that Monday's biopsy was negative and the lump under my left arm is a simple cyst, which needs no further attention or treatment. I really didn't realize how anxious I had been until he spoke those wonderful words: "It's benign." Then I realized I'd been emotionally holding my breath these past two days, scared to think or even breathe, lest I lose control and unravel into so much tangled yarn, like most of my failed knitting projects.

"Yes, Andrew, it is a rollercoaster ride," I answered him. And that's the truth. The past two days had been a sea of emotions carried on waves of hope and troughs of anxiety, just like the rollercoasters I rode when I was younger. The simplest little symptom which one would normally dismiss now carries the potential threat of cancer out of control and life turned topsy-turvy again. I know to expect this, and yet, in the midst of the scare, it's still a rollercoaster ride.

Today, Lord God, you have blessed my bold prayer for mercy. The biopsy is benign. Thank you for fulfilling my hope for more time with my husband and precious sons. Thank you that I dare hope to see Andrew graduate dental school. Thank you that I can reasonably dream of playing with my grandchildren one day, just as I played with my boys not so very long ago. I know I'm blessed beyond many women: I raised my sons to adulthood, and I am very grateful. I am also grateful for the abundance of your blessing, one more day cancer-free. Thank you, Great Physician. Forgive me for seeming greedy. Should you take me home tomorrow, my life has been rich and full. And if you leave me here on earth another year or ten, I pray I'll use the days wisely for your glory and service. Either way, I'm blessed and grateful to my Gracious God and Savior. What an anniversary present, God! You pick the best gifts!

A Different Beach Experience

I had my fifth treatment on Wednesday, June 16, and it really wiped me out. Ward and I had planned to leave for the beach on Saturday, but I just didn't have the energy to get myself together to pack and leave town. I dreaded five hours of car riding. So we left Sunday morning, late, and leisurely drove to the condo.

It's been a truly boring week so far. I am hesitant to go out to dinner anywhere because there are always crowds of people at the beach this time of year. Even with a reservation, the restaurants are crowded and I definitely don't want any germs. Ward is patient and very understanding. He runs, he walks on the beach and he sits on the balcony and enjoys the sun and the scenery. I sit in the condo, seeking shade and comfort from the sweltering heat of a summer that started out to be one of the hottest on record. I hear that at home, the temps reach into the 100's and I am thankful to be where it's only in the low 90's–but hot is hot and especially when one is wearing a wig. It's like wearing snow gear in the middle of this heat wave. So mostly, I work puzzles and knit in the comfort of the air conditioner with a bandana scarf tied over my naked head. I'm also reading, about a book a day, mostly fiction which is a rare choice of reading material for me. I suppose it's an escape from my current life.

I tried walking on the beach early Tuesday morning with a nice wide brimmed hat to shelter my face, and tons of sunscreen to protect me from any little ray of sunshine, even though it was only 8:00 AM. Still, it was muggy and hot, and after about 45 minutes of walking in God's beachside sauna, I was ready for the air conditioner. I've always hated to sweat–it makes me itch–and that hasn't changed with chemo.

One thing has changed, though. I've discovered that mosquitoes don't like the blood of chemo patients. I've always been one who was attacked by hordes of mosquitoes as soon as I walked out the door. Not so this year; they don't come near! Back home, when I go out to the pond, I would always cover myself with insect repellent, but chemo has proven to be a very effective repellent. Unfortunately, it's a very severe treatment for mosquito repellent! It also repels hair and taste buds, and creates lots of other challenges for the person who takes the chemo hit! Still, no mosquito bites is a small blessing in a challenging season of life.

June 24, Thursday

Who Is This Irritable Woman?

"Why are you being like this?" Ward asks in response to some short answer I have given to an innocent question he asked me. "You seem irritable. Is anything wrong?"

"Oh, I don't know, Ward!" I snap back. "I am irritable! Maybe it's the fact that I'm at the beach in sweltering heat, with a bald head that must be covered when I go out. I don't feel well from my chemo treatment, and I'm practically a prisoner in this condo! I'm not much of a beach person anyway, and now I can't even go to a theater or dinner or any of the things I usually do to amuse myself down here. Those seem like reasons enough to me to be irritable! And on top of that, now the rest of my eyelashes and eyebrows are falling out! I hate my life right now!"

This is the second time I recall being short and irritable with Ward for no fault of his own following a chemo treatment. It's like I wake up angry and frustrated and irritable and eager for this phase of my life to be over. I've about had it with being a chemo patient. I'm worn out and feel caught in limbo between human and guinea pig. I'm living this year of cancer and chemo treatments and don't even know if the treatments are doing any good. Furthermore, I don't know what permanent damage they may be doing. I don't even know if these two additional treatments will be effective or make any difference at all. And my doctor doesn't know either, because they are all making their best guesses in treating a disease which still wins the battle way too many times.

I must watch for a pattern to my emotions. Like most other symptoms and side effects of chemo, this irritable phase seems to follow a predictable timetable. Sometime about a week after treatment, I feel like I've turned into a raging pit bull. Perhaps what I need is a good dog handler! Certainly Ward is too kind and caring to deserve being married to a mad dog.

My eyelashes and eyebrows are definitely going and I feel
violated. They have been fine and nearly normal through
the previous four treatments. They thinned some, but were
still there. Now I'm getting large naked patches and I fear
within a short time they will all be gone. Why, after the fifth
treatment, would they come out now? It doesn't seem fair and
I feel injured. Not angry with God, but wounded. Wounded
by the treatment? Unjustly stripped of even more of myself?
By whom? I can't even answer these questions, but it feels
like the final assault. Hadn't I lost enough already? Head hair,
boobs–gone. The ability to feel in my chest, and underarm, and
even down the inside and back of my left arm, compromised
or absent. "I already gave at the office!" I want to cry out to the
unseen, unknown fiend who robs me now of the last little bit of
normalcy I enjoyed above my waist.

Only it's not really an unknown fiend. It's the effects of
chemotherapy, modern medicine's best efforts to save my life, to
rid me of an ugly disease. And it's not just above the waist that
I'm losing the rest of my hair–most of my pubic hair is gone,
too. I remember a funny story a friend shared about losing her
pubic hair during chemo. Apparently it's some of the last hair
to go. She was chatting with her husband as she pulled on her
wig and said, "It's funny that I haven't lost pubic hair since I've
lost the rest of my hair." He looked at her kind of funny for a
moment, and then replied, "You can't see down there, can you?"
She hadn't noticed that the last patch of hair she thought she
possessed had quietly exited her body. They had a good laugh.

But I am not laughing about this last loss. I feel naked and
exposed, bare skin over bone, muscle and fat. Why couldn't
some of the fat have gone, too? That's another insult of this kind
of chemo. It tends to make one gain weight! How incredibly
rude! I should have at least been able to come out of this a little
slimmer. But no! I seem to gain about a pound each treatment
cycle. I would scream, "It's not fair!" But who ever said anything

about fair? I am continually reminded of other sweet women before me who have suffered the indignities of chemo and cancer. Some are cured, some are in remission, and some are in eternity. Cancer is no respecter of persons, and chemo plays by its own rules. But it did sneak up on me with this late stage attack on the few hairs I had left and I am caught unprepared in its ambush.

I must remember that it's not attractive for big girls to whine. What's that cute saying? Oh, yes: "Put on your big girl panties and stop crying." I must get my big girl panties if only I can remember where I put them! That's another little side effect of chemo. I find that I am searching more frequently these days for particular words or names that escape my mind. Or I'll think that I need to do something, and then it goes out of my mind before I remember to do it. My doctor warned me that this phase might come, and I was worried about it because I once fancied myself to have a good mind. I thought of myself as a thinker. Really?

I was in a conversation recently with a friend, searching for some elusive word or thought, and said "I guess it's just chemo brain. My doctor said this could happen, and I hope it clears up when I'm done with chemo."

My slightly older friend laughed. "It's not chemo brain, Carolyn, and it's probably not going away! Its just life as you get older–get used to it!"

She's probably right. I've actually always been somewhat forgetful but at least right now I have an excuse to hang it on, so spare me the reality check, dear friend, while I pretend I'm not quietly losing my mind!

Andrew and Christin will be here tonight and I'm looking forward to some extra company. Andrew will run on the beach with Ward, and by next week I'll be in a safe place, chemo-wise, to venture out to shopping expeditions and dinner in restaurants. We'll go places where we can get reservations and spare me the lines of waiting in compressed crowds and I will feel better. I'm usually in a good mood on my third week post chemo because I feel physically better, and I know that my immune system is less compromised during this time. Still I am careful to avoid germs and crowds because I don't want anything to throw my treatment schedule off track. And while I await week three, I will make an extra effort to be kind to Ward who is also living a rather boring existence as I go through chemo.

Lord God my Father, please in all my irritability and forgetfulness, don't let me forget you. But even if I do, I am confident of this: You will not forget me. Of this I can be sure. Even if my mind should crumble away one thought after another, bit by bit, until I don't even know myself, you will still remember me and in paradise, my mind and my eyelashes will be restored, along with anything else I may have lost along the way. Thank you that you are strong enough to hold all the thoughts and the pieces of life which I have scattered and squandered along my journey, as well as those which simply splintered from the pressure of living in a broken world. Thank you that you are the Great Physician who inhabits both sides of eternity. Thank you that you will put all the broken pieces back together again. You, Heavenly Father, can accomplish for me what all the king's horses and all the king's men couldn't do for poor Humpty Dumpty. You alone can put me back together again. Good night, Daddy.

June 25, Friday

Goodbye Last Eyelashes

Most of my eyelashes are gone from the right side of my face along with most of that right eyebrow, and about half of their left twins are gone, too. So I'm sporting a lopsided, naked face, although it was never all that symmetrical anyway! I'm trying to learn to apply false eyelashes and that is an exercise in frustration! I should have taken a theatrical make-up class during my college years. I think I spent about 30 frustrating minutes on my first attempt to get those lashes attached to my eyelids–it must get easier than this! I called Tracy for some pointers and was shocked to learn one can only wear a pair of fake eyelashes about three times before the potential for eye infection sets in. At that rate, I calculate I'll be spending about $30 - $40 per month on lashes. So this exceeds the money I'm saving on haircuts. Furthermore, the time I was saving by not having hair to style or legs to shave is also more than consumed by the time it takes to fashion eyebrows and apply lashes. Oh, the costs of beauty in a broken world!

On the up side, Andrew and Christin are here, and this is my safe week from an immunity standpoint. I can feel comfortable shopping and eating out–yeah! And by the time I get home, I'll have only one more chemo session to endure. I'll be happy to be home where my boundaries are expanded and I have more things to occupy my time and mind within the confines of my home. By the time we come to the beach again, I can theoretically swim in the pool or splash in the ocean without fear of germs. I can go to a movie and not worry about the enclosed space breathing other peoples' air. We will take in a show at the Carolina Opry and stand in line at Ward's favorite cafeteria without worrying that some contagious person will cough their plague on me or my food.

Lord God, thank you that I have a future to look forward to with the wonderful husband you have given me. A few months ago, I feared I might be planning a fall funeral, or at least living out my last few months on Earth. I'm grateful for treatment options that offer the potential for a long future and another summer at the beach when I'll have hair and eyelashes–and nice implants to fill out my swimsuit top. Thank you that you are a God of hope. Thank you for the words of the prophet Jeremiah: "I know the plans that I have for you" says the Lord. "Plans to bless you and not harm you, plans to give you hope and a future."[4] You are my future, Lord God, both here and in eternity, and for whatever days I have left on Earth, thank you. Help me to use them wisely and well.

---

4   *Jeremiah 29:11*

Chapter 7: JULY
Finally, Chemo is Finished!

July 7, Wednesday

The Last Chemo Treatment

Today was my last chemo treatment. I was very much aware of this fact as I walked into the cancer treatment center. My doctor asked me if I was doing the happy dance and I think I told her I would be doing it when I'm done. But the truth of the matter is that I still have to go through a couple of weeks of the effects of this last treatment. I still have to practice the form of isolation I have prescribed for myself until I reach that third safe week. So my happy dance will actually be delayed until this last waltz with chemo is done. It's a slow dance now, and then I'll dance the exuberant, celebratory happy dance; oh, with gladness I'll dance that happy dance, Doctor. I'll dance with joy and thanksgiving!

My last walk out of the doors of the chemo unit was a bit anticlimactic. I had read magazines and worked Sudoku while the poison infused. Now I walked calmly to my car to await the inevitable side effects. No bells rang, no heavenly music played. The hot Richmond sun still beat down on my head–my hot, wig-clad head. I drove home, thankful to be done with the treatment, and anxious for the next two weeks to pass.

Heat Wave

Wearing a wig in Richmond's sweltering summer of heat and humidity is a challenging, and sometimes comic experience. I probably looked really entertaining recently as I zipped around town on those stop and go errands women sometimes do. I'm talking about those adventures when the car never has time to cool between shops and stops. It's just in and out of a heated metal box as one drives a few blocks between destinations. I stayed sweaty (actually, Southern gals don't sweat, we glisten), glistening all afternoon. I discovered that if I turned all the air conditioning vents on me, and then held the edges of my wig away from my head at stoplights, I could get a good little ventilation draft circulating around my glistening head. I must look funny to any neighboring drivers who happen to glance my way. But honestly, it just feels so good!

July 15, Thursday

Listing Symptoms

Today I decided to list the various symptoms I have experienced on this four-month journey through chemo. It seemed a good idea to keep this record should I have any health issues in the future that might be tied to this time in my life. I was surprised to identify 17 different ones. Thank God I did not experience all of them at the same time. Because they appeared a few each cycle of treatment, in varying degrees of intensity and spread over each three-week cycle, I never had a sense of so many different ones. It is blissful to be ignorant sometimes, and as I looked back over the course of treatment I was glad I had been unaware of so many different physical challenges.

It would be way too boring to list them all here, but I do recall that before treatment started, I worried about the possibility of numbness and tingling in my hands and feet; a common effect of chemo. In fact, I did not recognize that symptom until into the fifth cycle. It may have been present before, but I often miss symptoms early on. I just don't seem to be terribly aware of small changes in my body. It's not until something is quite obvious that I usually notice. That probably makes the fact that I was so quick to identify the breast pain that pushed me to early detection even more miraculous than I already think it is.

At any rate, regarding the numbness and tingling, I worried that I wouldn't be able to use my hands for the many crafts I enjoy. Once again, I have been blessed. These symptoms are most noticeable in my feet and the two smallest fingers on my left hand. Those fingers are more likely symptoms of nerve damage from the lymph nodes removed from under my left arm for testing. The fingers work fine, they just feel a little odd, but that's OK. I can still sew and have been able to do whatever I want with that hand. My feet still take me wherever I want to go, and sometimes they don't even know they're going there! That could be a big bonus when I cram them in to shoes that are cute but would be torturous if my feet knew they hurt. But I just won't tell them. "What they don't know won't hurt them" is my motto! Of course I'll be careful not to let them blister or bleed.

July 19, Monday

Moving On

Now begins my upward swing following chemo. I can start living my normal life again–church, CBS, shopping, movies, with no anxiety about danger around every crowd. This Sunday I'll start back to church, I'll see Tracy's kids; maybe Ward and I will take in a movie. No longer will I see crowds and kids as my personal potential suicide bomber. I've already sent out an email telling friends I'm going to be collecting hugs, making up for all those hugs I've declined in the past four months. I'm really looking forward to going out without imagining every surface as a germ field to be navigated carefully.

On a more disappointing note, I've lost all of my eyelashes and eyebrows now, a real disappointment since I made it through four treatments with these facial adornments mostly intact. I have gotten very good at drawing in eyebrows, and I can put on eyelashes with relative ease. Still, it takes some time to do and I have to plan my morning and evening make-up and cleansing routines around my fake eyelashes. Who knew such a small thing could take so much attention? I realize that many women going through chemo don't worry about these small things and most people probably don't notice that one's eyelashes are missing, especially if other eye make-up is well applied. But I feel naked without my eyelashes and yearn to feel normal in a surreal time of life. I choose to invest the extra time for the joy of seeming normal. It's all about perception—mine!

July 23, Friday

It's All Fake

Today I hosted the Butterflies, my longtime prayer partners who have met and prayed together for the past twenty years. As always, at some point the conversation turns to me and the ways I am coping with the changes in my body. "Honey, everything above my waist is fake," I joked with one of them.

In fact, there is a lot of fake stuff on my exterior, but my heart, O Lord, I pray my heart is real, so very real because of this ordeal. I pray my spirit has been softened, molded to be more like my Savior. While the outside is a lot of smoke and mirrors, please Lord, let my inside be purified, even in the fires and floods of cancer and chemo. Most importantly, thank you that you have walked with me through this trial.

Chapter 8: AUGUST
New Direction

August 16, Monday

Is That Hair?!

August marked a new stage in my cancer-chemo journey. My hair started growing back on my head, in the fourth week following my last chemo treatment, just as the oncologist predicted. I had already been searching for the first sprigs of fluff into the third week post treatment, an intense search of my scalp with the aid of my magnifying mirror and an extra pair of glasses. It's a wonder the piercing intensity of my gaze didn't burn off any little hairs which dared venture forth!

I first spotted tiny hairs popping up sparsely on my head like bits of fluff, much like a newborn's fuzzy head. In fact, I looked a lot like my son Andrew's four-month-old baby picture; that is if you ignore the contrast between baby skin and the skin of a sixty year old. Often these first new hairs were preceded by little dimple-like indentions in the scalp. I found myself staring in my magnifying mirror each evening for several minutes at a time, admiring the new growth and willing my hair to grow faster, and thicker, and longer. After all, I joked, it all fell out in six days. Shouldn't it come back in with the same speed? But in fact, it will probably take about six months to be nice enough to go wigless: that's one month's growth for every day of shedding. That hardly seems fair! In fact, as I still see patches of baldness into this third week of growth, I'm silently praying I will not end up with lifelong patches of shiny hairless circles in my head.

The first couple of weeks found me frequently snatching off my wig to scratch my itchy head with all the digits of both hands and if I could have gotten my toes up to my head, I would have used them too. My head seemed to itch constantly, whether from the new hair growth or the incessant sweating (oh, excuse me, *glistening*) born of this hot Richmond summer. At any rate, it finally dawned upon me to follow my daily shower with a small dab of hair conditioner to my sparse little hair farm and the itching seems to have subsided. Whether the conditioner did the trick, or perhaps the slight drop in temperature, I no longer feel like the great ape I feared I was becoming.

I celebrated when my eyebrows started filling in shortly after my hair began coming back, but last week I got quite a shock. More eyelashes fell out. And the eyebrows which were growing last week are strangely absent today. "Wait a minute, I need those things!" I want to scream to the unknown eyebrow fairy who apparently secrets away my lashes and brows in my sleep. She must be sister to the tooth fairy, but at least that sibling leaves a reward for the expectant children who carefully place their tooth treasures under their pillows. I get no reward from this brow fairy; in fact, I think she is quite diabolical. And besides, what does an eyelash fairy do with all those missing hairs? Who needs these brows and lashes more than me?

Yesterday after church, I was encircled by a half dozen women, mostly members of the sisterhood of the pink ribbon, or at least that's what I've named those sweet breast cancer survivors who came to comfort and encourage me when news of my diagnosis got out last winter. So I pelted them with questions about hair and eyelashes and eyebrows. And I'm not entirely happy with their answers. Some never got full lashes and brows back. Some didn't pay that much attention in the first place. Hair for some is still curly three years post treatment and some are back to their pre-cancer styles a year later. So the bottom line seems to be this: No one can predict exactly what someone's experience will be. Hair may or may not grow back; same for eyelashes and brows. The kind of hair which returns after chemo can be a surprise, too. I'm starting to be weary of surprises.

A couple of weeks ago, one of Ward's patients said, "Tell your wife her hair will probably grow back curly, but it usually goes back to normal after a year or so. But it will probably come it white, and she'll just have to get used to that."

"Oh, my wife won't be getting used to white. She knows exactly what color her hair will be," my husband assured her. "She already has the box of hair dye ready." Ward is correct. My hair may come back thin or patchy or curly, but I'm positive it won't be white. I may choose some new shade of brown or red or blonde–but I definitely will not choose white or gray!

Lord God, thank you that you've permitted me to live in a time when there are lots of cosmetic options for women. I can choose to define external beauty in a way that brings me peace and joy. You, however, have defined inner beauty for all your daughters. "Your beauty should be that of your inner self, the unfading beauty of a gentle and quiet spirit, which is of great worth in God's sight."[1] Please help me to adorn my inner self with the traits you find beautiful, Sweet Jesus.

---

1   *I Peter 3:3-4*

August 17, Tuesday

Permanent Implants

Thursday can't come soon enough for me. I'll enter the hospital early that morning to have my tissue expanders removed and permanent silicone implants placed. I'll also shed the port that ferried chemo from the IV bags into my body. I'm grateful for the medical function both foreign objects performed, but I'm more grateful to have them removed. I'm happy to move on to what I hope will be a life with cancer and its chemo cousin gone for good.

It's another "Come Monday" week for me. By next Monday, I anticipate feeling much better than I likely will feel this Friday. I've learned to welcome Mondays on this journey and I don't think many people can say they honestly welcome Mondays. But a bout with a scary illness, or any threatening life event, is the great bender of perspectives. I hope my perspectives have bent toward the good. Monday is a symbolic reminder to me of hope for new beginnings. Although Sunday is technically the first day of the week, it's also the end of the weekend and Monday signals fresh beginnings for me.

In fact, how many new diets, new jobs, and new projects have I started on Monday? Probably most of the ones I ever started. Well, this Monday, I'll be well on my way to healing from this reconstructive surgery. No longer battling cancer, I'm now starting to feel like a survivor of that enemy; I'm a woman who looks forward to the day I'll feel I beat the odds. I'll bet it will be a Monday. In fact, wouldn't it be delightful if one Monday I see eyelashes and eyebrows back in their rightful places! Come Monday, maybe.

In the meantime, I do have things to celebrate. When I saw my plastic surgeon a couple of weeks ago, she permitted me to have one more saline injection, expanding the space where the implants will dwell. I left her office so happy about that, because I feel more balanced, more whole with a chest a little larger than the one I lost. Now there will hopefully be room for implants closer to what I hoped for when this process began. So, if I never get my eyelashes back, at least I'll have my mini-Dollys. Maybe they'll be distractions enough that the missing lashes won't be noticeable!

Thank you, God, for letting me amuse myself in these fanciful thoughts. I know it's all silly, but you are the one who created women, and you certainly used your creativity when you made me! Are you still chuckling? Well, I'm laughing right along with you! Thank you for giving me a sense of humor, even if it's twisted sometimes. Thank you for letting me find a reason to grin, even where some might think my circumstances grim. I think I have a lot to look forward to. And I'm determined to find the fun along the way. For now, I'm having fun thinking I'll look great when all this process is over. And if I think I look great, but don't really, I know the folks who love me will compliment me and love me just the way I am. I'm grateful that your love is like that, too, Lord.

In fact, I'm reminded of an experience I had a few weeks ago when my neighbor, Peter, dropped in unexpectedly. Everyone but Peter uses my front door, but he and Carole lived beside us from the time we moved into this house as newlyweds until they moved to a country home place too many seasons ago– actually about two years ago, I think. At any rate, Peter uses the French door at the side of my house. As I sat typing on the computer, Peter tapped on the door beside it. There I sat in a bandana scarf, no eyebrows painted on, no false eyelashes glued to my nearly naked lids, and no make-up coloring my pale cheeks or lips. To me, I look like death warmed over when I am that undone.

I apologized, embarrassed, about how bad I looked and told Peter I don't even answer the front door in this state.

Fortunately, he didn't come to the front door because he was locked out of his unsold home beside us and he needed the spare key I keep carefully hidden in my place. He said, "Carolyn, people who love you don't even notice whether or not you have on make-up or a wig. They see your heart, the real Carolyn. You needn't worry about such things, because people who care about you just want to be with you." Then he told me the story of another minister he had once known who was also missing hair and brows and lashes, not from cancer but from some other cruel twist of life on a broken planet. But Peter said once people knew him, they didn't even notice any more that these expected characteristics were missing because they had come to love the man. They saw his heart and hardly noticed the absent hair.

It was another version of the Velveteen Rabbit, which a friend used to introduce me as a speaker years before, when I had long hair, a skinny waist (well, skinnier than it is now!) and plenty of eyelashes to hold my mascara. It was another reminder that I tend to judge myself much more harshly than I would judge others. If I had a friend in my situation, just as Peter did for me, I would speak words of encouragement and assurance–and mean them, just as he did. I don't care if my friends have hair or not; I simply enjoy the presence of their company, the wisdom of their words, and the joy of their laughter. I don't know why I am so hard on myself when I am so willing to extend mercy and grace to others. I must do something about that. After all, God has poured out his mercy and grace upon me; shouldn't I model my Father's example? *I'll try to work on that Lord, because I know you intended me to be more than eyelashes and long hair. I'll work on that. And maybe you'll help me bend my perspective just a little bit more toward your pleasure, come Monday.*

August 18, Wednesday

I've Got Cancer Again!?!!

I really, really hope this doesn't develop into a continuing pattern! I got my third cancer diagnosis today. That's one every eight months since last summer, and I'm about ready to move on to some other, more edifying adventure. This one isn't scary, really; annoying would be a better word for it. I have a superficial basal cell cancer on my left leg. It's a spot I've watched for a long time, and mentioned it to my doctors on several occasions. Even at this six-month check-up visit with my dermatologist, she thought it was nothing. However, because I was concerned, she biopsied it, assuring me even as she cut that she was confident it was nothing. Then, the telephone rang today. "Mrs. Mustian, we got the lab work back on your biopsy from last week. It's nothing serious, just a superficial basal cell skin cancer, but we need to get you back in here to treat it." One thing I know for sure: if it worries me, it must be biopsied. I've been right three times when professionals assured me there was nothing to be concerned about.

Of course when it comes to these basal cell cancers, I'll bet at least 50% of the fair-skinned people around my age have these little cancers. Most of us baked ourselves in baby oil when we were teens, craving that illusive golden California tan. We didn't all get the action we hoped for from the sun, but are we ever getting action now! "No thank you," I want to say, "I've already had two other helpings of cancer, I'll just pass on this one." But of course it's not as easy as passing dishes at a big family dinner. This is more like "duck, duck, goose", and I keep ending up the goose.

Thankfully, though, this news comes on a day that has been a wonderful one for me. I spent a couple of hours this morning with Gwen, who was, and still is, the assistant teaching director at the Powhatan Bible Study where I substituted last fall. She has been a continual blessing and dear friend. We sipped coffee and caught up on the months since we were last together. Time-lapses really make no difference between kindred spirits; we pick up where we left off. I look forward to visiting the Powhatan class this fall.

This afternoon was a surprise beyond surprises. My arborist came to advise me on a tree which had developed mysterious holes. I feared some lethal insect infestation but it was much simpler than that. A yellow nut hatcher had drilled its methodically placed holes up and down the trunk, but in straight lines, a signature calling card for that creature. No real harm done and the tree doesn't have to be taken down; I'm happy about that. But that was not the surprise. He and I got into a long discussion about life issues and God and dealing with cancer. And it all started because I mentioned that I had been on chemo this summer, wearing a wig in the scorching summer heat wave.

That opened the door for an amazing conversation, which the Lord God used to bless both of us far beyond what we had either one expected on a simple tree evaluation. I think we both were spiritually edified. It's another picture of God using a challenging situation in my life to give me an opportunity to be a blessing to someone else, and to also be blessed in return. I wonder how many blessings I've missed over the years because I was reticent to expose a small chink in my armor. I've always been so busy keeping that strong, protective shield in place. I've worked so hard at this chemo thing to look "normal" and hide this particular challenge to my life. And yet, when I open the door to my humanity just a tiny crack, God rushes in to fill it with blessings overflowing.

I am reminded of a book I read once, many years ago, called "Sent to be Vulnerable." The author's premise was that God means for us to open our hearts and souls and be real with one another. Today, two real people stood in my yard and shared from their hearts–and one of them was me. Yes, Carolyn, you can still be real, even in false eyelashes, and penciled brows and synthetic wigs. And early tomorrow morning, I'm going to get my permanent fake boobs, too! But underneath those silicone implants beats a real heart for God. *Help me keep it real, Lord Jesus, help me keep it real.*

August 30, Monday

I'm a Hero?

"You're my hero! You're my hero!" the nurse kept telling me as she led me from my doctor's waiting room to the exam room. I was dressed as I usually am when I come to the doctor: hair styled, make-up applied, nice clothes. I had been in surgery the day before as my plastic surgeon removed the rock-hard expanders and replaced them with soft, more natural feeling permanent silicone implants: "The largest they make," she said, although I doubt that because I've seen the Hollywood gals and I'm nowhere near some of their sizes.[2]

Nevertheless, I wanted to be more proportional to the rest of my generous body than I had been with my God-given breasts, so big was good for me. Now, the day following surgery, I was back in her office because both of my drains were leaking. I had been soaking through several gauze sponges every few hours. I felt like a woman on a period, only this flow was coming out from under my arms!

"Why do you keep saying I'm your hero?" I asked the nurse.

"Look at you!" she exclaimed. "You look great. And didn't you have to go to the ER yesterday afternoon, too? Did you drive yourself here today?"

---

2   *In fact, they were the largest that brand makes and I'm actually delighted with my new look.*

"Yes, I did go back to the ER yesterday because one of the drain sites was leaking, but of course it had stopped by the time we arrived. And no, I didn't drive, but I think I could have. My husband's off work today, so he drove me." I answered. "I really feel fine, though. I'm only taking Tylenol. "

I had taken a Percocet at bedtime of the surgical day, mostly to be sure I fell asleep easily, but I didn't need one the next morning. I bathed, dressed and put on my usual make-up, including eyelashes and wig. I accented my outfit with jewelry, like I do most every day. This day was no different. It was flattering to be complimented by someone who sees post-ops routinely, but I have learned over time that my body accommodates to surgery pretty well in the pain department. Unfortunately, I seem to have had my run of annoyances following surgery, and this was no different. For whatever reason, both of my drains were leaking, so my doctor had to take additional stitches around each opening to stop the blood. I also learned I have the distinction of being the only patient she's had with double leaking drains, too. Of course. Sigh. Why am I not surprised?

Drains Out

"Remind me to put numbing cream on you before we remove these stitches," the doctor said when she sewed the extra stitches. A week later, when the stitches were snipped to remove the first drain, I did remind her. And I again reminded her nurse two days later when the second drain came out. The drain removals were pretty easy and relatively uneventful for me. For the first one, I felt nothing. For the second one, I could feel the long tube snaking out of my body, not a painful feeling, just weird. I was actually pretty excited about having that much feeling, because that was on the left side, which had a bit more surgery than the right. *Thank you, Jesus, for making the way easy for me one more time. And thanks for whatever amount of sensation you chose to restore in this broken body.* I knew I was fortunate to have these particular drains because there's another kind that has a square shape inside the body that holds it in place, and is leak proof. But it is more uncomfortable coming out, according to some of the other women I've talked with. The stitches weren't really painful, so all in all, I think I came out ahead.

The most annoying thing about the post op period before the drains came out was the fact that I couldn't shower. Birdbaths from sink basins get old really quickly and I was thrilled when I could finally hop back in the shower. I just stood there several minutes letting the water flow over my moisture-thirsty skin, and it felt marvelous! I take so much for granted.

Finding comfortable clothing is another interesting issue. My doctor prescribes a sleep bra round the clock during the healing process, but my sensitive skin gets itchy from the elastic band around the bottom, even though it's covered by the cotton/synthetic fabric from which the bra is made. Furthermore, I get itchy from any clothing tight on my skin so I sometimes look like a flea-infested creature as I try to scratch under the offending garment. In her graciousness to accommodate me, my doctor said I could wear any kind of bra I want to, and I've tried a couple of other ones. But what I want to wear when I sleep is nothing tight around my chest. I'm wearing bras, though, because I don't want these new puppies to stretch! (Can implants stretch? I don't know, and I don't want to be my own test case!)

Wednesday, I'll go in for my two-week check-up and I'm looking forward to it. For one thing, I have these really hard lumps under each arm, right above the bra line, and I suspect that fluid collects there for some unknown reason. I'm tempted to ask if I can wear a bustier. I notice that when I wore the ace bandage the two days prescribed after the last drain was removed, the hard spots softened somewhat overnight. In fact, I wore the ace again last night because after wearing a different bra yesterday, I had **two** ridges under each arm–the new ridge appeared above the top of the skinny side strap of the bra I had chosen for my V-necked dress.

Maybe what I need is that elastic body suit on infomercials, which air in the wee hours of the morning. I see them advertised in the middle of the nights when I awake for no good reason. They claim to reduce a woman's dress size by one or two sizes, but actually, I think their fat is all compressed into the chest area where their breasts appear to become rockets lying on a shelf, awaiting launch. I certainly don't want to launch my new chest art out into the floor!

I have continued my daily hair vigil, watching my head hair grow for several minutes at a stretch, nearly every night, and sometimes in the mornings, too, if I'm not in a rush to make some appointment or another. It never looks much different from day to day, except that I do notice a few new hairs popping up from time to time. I do recognize change over several days. I can also see that it is getting thicker–with the word *thicker* being a relative term. I still need lots more hairs before I pass from functionally bald to wigless wonder. Although lots of people have warned me to expect curly hair, I hadn't seen any signs of it even up to the end of last week.

This weekend I was too busy to keep hair vigil. I was in the kitchen most of Saturday as I prepared lunch for about a dozen of Dave's Virginia Tech friends who were helping celebrate his 22nd birthday at his new condo in Blacksburg. When I learned Andrew could have dinner with us Saturday night, I cooked more chicken and potato salad to give him a preview dinner of my next day's menu since he couldn't travel with us for the celebration. After a day of cooking, cleaning, cooking, cleaning, eating, cleaning, I fell into bed without a glance at my hair (well, head, really, there's not a lot of hair yet). Sunday morning I was up early to bathe, apply makeup, eyelashes, and all the things that make me look normal. I packed dress clothes for dinner at the Hotel Roanoke on Sunday evening. I packed food for the lunch celebration and we were on the road by 8 AM. My hair was not noticeably different yesterday morning. It looked pretty much the same as I removed eyelashes and makeup last night before I melted into my welcoming new bed last night. (We just bought a mechanical bed with a Swedish foam mattress–ahh!)

So imagine my surprise when I looked into my magnifying mirror this morning–the same mirror I use every day to perform hair inspection, along with my brow and lash seek and search mission. "Oh, my goodness!" I exclaimed to no one but myself. Even my cat has grown tired of my laborious morning routine and she had already deserted her post. "My hair got curly over night!" And indeed it had!

I don't even understand the process, but all the little hairs that were straight just two days ago are curly now, including some that are nearly an inch long. Those long ones are some of the hair that didn't fall out during the chemo process. Go figure. And here's the added joy. I'm pretty sure I see a few–maybe three–little eyelashes peeping through the skin. I hope these baby eyelashes see those fake lashes and are spurred to compete for length and/or fullness. And I hope they stay in the eyelid this time. My eyebrows make a show of growing new brow hairs, but they never seem to mature. I see tiny hairs, maybe 1/16th of an inch, but all the mature lashes are gone now, and the lashes, which started in last month, disappeared over night some weeks ago. I'm hopeful, but cautiously so. I just don't want to be disappointed again and again. I'm trying to assure myself that I can live without eyebrows and eyelashes if I have to, and of course I can–I just don't want to. But as my mother used to say, "You're big enough for your wants not to hurt you."

Lord, make me big enough. I know there are people who have lost way more than eyebrows and eyelashes and I'm really trying to be a big girl about this. After all, my legs still work, so do my eyes, and my hands and feet and my ears. I'm very blessed. I know this. And I've gotten very good with my camouflage equipment. So please look the other way while I whine about insignificant things like eyebrows and eyelashes. I'm trying not to be ungrateful for your many blessings and I truly am thankful for all you've done for me, including giving me great makeup and the ability to use it. AMEN! (I'm done whining for the moment, you can turn back around now, God.) I'm so glad God is big enough for my wants not to hurt him, or me, either for that matter! Amen, again.

Chapter 9: SEPTEMBER
Back in the Groove

September 7, Tuesday

Quilts and Books and New Identity

I wasn't looking for a new pastime; I didn't need another project to distract my attention from the things I ought to be doing, like housework, and sewing my Dad some new slacks, or finishing the family photo albums I started re-working last summer. I just wanted a few books to read while I recovered from the reconstructive surgery. I'm not a fiction reader by habit, except when I go on vacation. On those times, I let my mind also take a vacation away from the weightier subjects that usually occupy my brain space. A mental vacation seemed like a good idea post-op, so I headed off to my neighborhood branch of the public library.

As I browsed the shelves of new releases, the friendly librarian began pointing out latest titles by authors who must be well known by those who usually choose fiction, but their names meant nothing to me. Nor did I have a good answer for him when he asked what type of fiction I usually enjoy. I don't usually enjoy fiction at all. He was trying to be helpful, but his questions made it even more clear that I was little girl lost in a place I seldom frequent. Finally I said, "I rarely read fiction, I'm just looking for a little diversion for a couple of weeks," and hoped I didn't sound snooty about reading choices.

I selected five books, which appeared to be widely different types, and headed home for the next day's surgery. Then I proceeded to read about a book a day, and went back the following week for a new supply. I was surprised by the variety in style of writing. Some books contained such simple plots, such underdeveloped characters, and such elementary words that I was surprised other adults read them. Some authors wrote with a magic pen–each sentence danced with beauty and challenged me to pay attention and drink in every delicious word. With one author, I didn't even care what she was writing about, her prose was so beautiful I wanted more, so I hurried back to the library before I had even finished her newest release to check out any others written by her. Happily I found one and snatched it greedily off the shelf as though I were in competition with others racing for her stories. One might suspect that fiction reading has become my new passtime, but that is not the case.

Among the books I chose was a rather simple story, read in a couple of easy hours. It was a tiny volume about a quilting club, the story woven in a setting where people came for quilting lessons and even quilting retreats and camps. I didn't dream such places exist, but they do. After reading her book, my grandmother's unfinished quilt top began to quietly sing to me from the bottom shelf of the closet where unfinished projects repose in my house. I went to the internet and discovered there's a wide world of quilts out there, including retreats and camps and stores galore. There are quilting tours where people spend a weekend driving from one quilt shop to the next crisscrossing several counties in their adventure. I began to imagine that I could actually make a quilt of my own, using my sewing machine, of course.

"I need to take a quilting class," I thought. My grandmother died in the early seventies and I became the owner of one of her unfinished quilts. I even pulled it out once, when the boys were just starting elementary school and in my naïveté I imagined that I would have time to take on some new activities for myself. I dreamed of myself peacefully quilting as I sat by the fire in the evenings, little boys quietly sleeping in their little beds. I found the only quilting store for miles around, took my quilt top in and selected fabric for finishing it. Another kindergarten mom was an accomplished quilter and she gave me some tips on how to quilt this piece, but somehow I just didn't do it. Part of the challenge was that my grandmother made all of her quilts by hand, stitch by tiny stitch, but machine quilting seemed to have replaced that laborious process, and I didn't own the huge quilting frames, which enjoyed a permanent spot in Granny's basement. Someone did clue me in that hoop quilting was a fine substitute for those giant wooden structures. I bought a set of hoops–but the task still seemed huge, and daunting. The unfinished quilt slept in my closet, and my dream of finishing my grandmother's quilt also slept–not so much the boys! Boys rarely sleep until Mom and Dad are exhausted and dreamless.

Fast forward a dozen and a half years. The boys sleep in other places now in dorms or rented apartments. I, after reading one simple, small book about quilting, couldn't stop thinking about quilts. Thank goodness the detective book I read didn't send me out to hunt criminals–or worse yet, try to commit the perfect crime! Nor did I want to rush out and find a secret lover after I completed the book about a middle-aged character who had an affair. But the quilting thing…I couldn't get it out of my mind.

I headed off to the quilt shop closest to my house according to the internet, determined to find a class. A lovely young woman took me in tow as I walked into the shop, no doubt thinking I looked like a kindergartner lost in a great big school. She led me to a list of potential classes, but they didn't fit my complex life schedule. She even offered to call the instructor and see if we could tailor two different sessions into one for me. Instead,

I settled on purchasing a how-to book called "Piecing the Piece of Cake Way." Talk about combining two loves: dessert and quilting! I reasoned that as a seamstress it would be easy enough to read the book, with its generous pictures, and hobble together some semblance of a quilt. I gathered small pieces of fabric, called "Fat Quarters", a fourth of yard of fabric cut into roughly a square which quilters collect like kids once collected baseball cards.

I gathered my newly purchased treasures and headed home to read and do quilting. I was totally hooked in about a minute. In a few days I had produced my first quilt, a baby-sized rectangle which I had decided would go to my cousin who is expecting her second child. Then I remembered another cousin whose second baby was born in July. Because she has a toddler as well, she really needed nothing for the new baby, and I have been agonizing over a good gift. Money seemed impersonal; gift cards just money in plastic. But a homemade quilt? Now that could be a treasure for a young woman who does not sew. I emailed her mom to inquire about colors and began collecting lavenders and purples–in fat quarters, of course.

I wasn't looking for a new hobby or another project to hijack my time. Yet I found a new passion, a new outlet for my creative bent. And I found so much more. Ever since I completed chemo, I've had a sense of waiting for the other shoe to drop. The doctors removed all the cancer from my body when I had surgery. My lymph nodes were clear. But my cancer was an aggressive type so I had to have chemo. It felt like I still had cancer and the side effects confirmed that I was a cancer victim. I only had to look in the mirror to see the devastation it had wreaked on my body: fake boobs, fake brows and lashes, two wigs. Plus, there's the waiting to see if it comes back. In three years, if I'm still cancer-free, my chances for long term survival greatly improve. But there's the waiting, the wondering, the doubts about whether I can make long distance plans for my life. As though any of us can, really, but if one doesn't have a potentially terminal illness, it is easier to imagine living into old age.

So, I've been marking time, counting off months in my head. I remember when my doctor said, at my last chemo treatment "Are you doing the happy dance today?" I smiled and said something appropriate, but my heart wasn't dancing. I still had to get through that cycle of treatment, but more importantly, I had to get through the next few years cancer-free. I didn't feel finished with cancer and my feet refused to dance.

Then I landed on quilting and it has become my happy dance. I have fun when I quilt. I feel a sense of accomplishment as I sew and when the last stitch is sewn, the last basting removed, I feel happy. I look at the new creation and see beauty. More importantly though, quilting is a new beginning for me. Everything else in my life is something I'm going back to doing again, something I did before cancer and chemo. Most of my life is picking up where I left off last January. But quilting is fresh and new–a different world entirely, and I have a new title. I was not a quilter and now I am. Instead of being altered by things lost, I'm recreated with something new, both to do and to be. I have a new skill, a new interest, a new identity. When I go into the quilting shop, I am not Carolyn-with-cancer, I'm Carolyn with her first quilt. I'm the new babe on the block hungry to take in all they can teach me. I'm the gal who picked up the quilt and left the cancer behind.

I have not known how to think of myself in terms of cancer. I hear the words *victim* and *survivor* attached to those who have done battle with this stealth disease. In the days that I stitched my first quilt, I left the world of chemo and cancer and sickness behind. I am neither a victim nor a survivor. I am well. "Look, Doctor, I'm doing my happy dance now. It's a little later than you expected it, but it's a joyous dance, and I'm smiling."

Lord God, there's a trite saying that's been kicked around for years, but it represents a truth nonetheless: God never closes a door unless he also opens a window. You gave me a new joy in quilting. It's much more than just a new skill, a new hobby, and a new distraction. Quilting marks a moment in time for me: the door has closed on cancer, and the window has opened to invite me into a new world of colors and designs and expressions of beauty. It's an explosion of possibilities. I no longer think of myself as a woman with cancer or a woman who was a victim and is a survivor of that disease.

Instead, I'm a woman with fabric and a plan, a needle and a cutting wheel—and I know how to use them! Thank you, God, for giving me fresh reason to smile. Thank you for giving me a visual picture of my new life post-cancer. Like my quilt, my life, my body has been patched back together by loving hands—my doctors, my nurses, my family, my friends—but most importantly, Lord God, I'm pieced back together by your loving hands, hands of the Amazing Creator. I am made into something I was not: I am a quilter.

And aren't you cool, Lord God Creator, to give me a little taste of new creation straight out of tiny swatches of fabric: more out of less, beauty out of pieces. You made Earth out of void, a world out of nothing. You still make new creations out of broken lives. Now you permit me to sample in a small way the joy of creation. From small snippets of cloth, some nearly useless scraps cast off in the bottom of my fabric chest, I create an explosion of orderly color with function that is more than its tiny parts. I'm a new creator of quilts. I'm still smiling and my heart is doing the happy dance!

September 9, Thursday

Melding New with Old

Oh what a lovely day! My Community Bible Study® class began leadership training this morning and I finally was reunited with some of the women who have prayed for me, written cards and notes, sent food, made phone calls and even visited me at home or in the hospital to keep me encouraged during the months of surgeries and chemotherapy. I was so happy to see everyone. More importantly, I was happy to be back doing something that felt customary and has been a major part of my life for the past twenty-two years. It was another step toward life that is familiar, like breathing. I was happy to gasp in great gulps of CBS atmosphere this morning where there are people whom I love and who love me as well.

I had worried a bit about feeling awkward walking back in after a seven-month hiatus, but it was made easier by the fact that these ladies had been out on summer break, too, just like me, so we were like school girls meeting up with friends we'd missed seeing over summer. We were all hugging one another, and I was no different than anyone else. I was well aware, however, that since I had last seen them, I had been through lots of physical changes. I knew at least some of them would steal sly glances at my chest area: I've seen that happen over and over again since the word of my mastectomies first got out. I made it no secret last winter that I planned to come out of this trauma well-endowed in the chest area. So I had a plan to help all of us over this awkward reunion.

I knew that we would do some sort of getting-to-know-you activity at the start of the morning, because always in the fall there are several gals new to leadership, and occasionally, they are even new to the Far West End study, having transferred from some other CBS class. Alice's instructions to us were to tell our name, our position in leadership, and something outside of Bible Study that we focused on this past year. As we moved around the table, some women mentioned hobbies, others their families, some spoke of a place or activity that captures their whole attention. Several mentioned that when they read a book, they get so involved in its pages that they lose perspective on children or family or other life responsibilities. It was a great segue for me when my turn came.

"As some of you know, this year for me was focused a lot on breast cancer," I began. I saw the look of shock and inevitable sadness or pity on the faces of some of the ladies new to leadership. "I tell you that because of what else I have to tell you this morning. When I was recovering from surgery a few weeks ago, I read a number of novels since I couldn't do much else for those first days, and like some of you, I got totally involved in the books. One was a book about quilting. When I'd finished reading it, I was hooked. I went into a quilting store, purchased a bunch of fabric and a how-to book, and sewed my first quilt last week. Now I have something else to show you. Alice didn't tell us to do a show and tell, but I brought one." I'm sure they expected me to whip out my new quilt. Instead I stood up, placed my hands on my hips as I pulled back the shirt, which gave modesty to my well-fitting tank top. "My surgery three weeks ago was to place my permanent implants, and I wanted you all to see them because, after all, you all prayed for these puppies!" And I sat back down. Now the looks of pity had turned to peals of laughter and I turned to the girl at my right, who was next up to introduce herself. I said, "Top that, Judy!" And the room erupted in laughter again.

My anxiety was broken and I hope theirs was too. By giving them permission to look, we could get that over with so that the next time I spoke to them, as a group or individually, they wouldn't feel like they had to sneak a peek to see if I looked "normal", whatever that is! I've never thought of normal when I think of my looks anyway, and many women are, like me, highly critical of their own perceived deficits in the appearance department. In fact, though, God has made each of us unique and wonderful. *Normal* has a broad definition across cultures and ages, but when someone falls outside of that broad norm, people sometimes can't help but look.

My scars and reconstruction are well hidden under clothing; still women worry about breast cancer. They worry that they might get it; they worry if they have it that they will never look feminine or normal. They wonder if they will ever move past it. I admit the latter feeling at times. But it's easy to cover my scars with pretty clothing and my plastic surgeon is doing a splendid job creating gorgeous chest art. Still, I can only image how hard life must be for people with disfiguring conditions like facial scars or crumpled bodies. People stare or determinedly look away to keep from staring rudely. They don't know where to look–or what to say. Furthermore, women are curious, like cats (and men are, too, they just don't get the bad rap we do!) probably because of the fear the word cancer produces in most of us. Better for me to face their curiosity immediately and move on.

Besides, I want my friends, old and new, to be aware that I'm working with a false front in more ways than one. If my wig is on crooked, someone needs to tell me. If one of my eyelashes crawls down my face and rests on my cheek like a lazy centipede, I want to be alerted. I carry eyelash glue, and friends don't let friends walk around unglued! I may be slightly unhinged in the mental department, but never let it be said that I am "glue-less"!

So I dropped my surprise on the unsuspecting new ladies and on old friends as well. Then later in the morning, I had a few surprises dropped on me by a loving heavenly Father who reminds me that I am more than a cancer survivor. I am part of God's new creation, renewed in Christ, rebuilt by my plastic surgeon and refreshed by my sisters in Christ at CBS. As we reviewed the calendar for the year, Alice, our Assistant Teaching Director, mentioned a retreat scheduled in February and held up a book called "Becoming a Woman of Influence". Great title, I thought, and I jotted it down in my notes. As I wrote, my heart did a little flutter and I thought, "I'd like to lead that retreat." Immediately, I chastised myself: *"Carolyn, Alice probably has some excellent speaker already lined up, and how presumptuous of you to even think you should lead that retreat!"* I shoved those thoughts out of my head, embarrassed at myself and feeling ashamed of what felt like ego on the loose.

Later that morning, during a break in the sessions, Alice grabbed my arm as I passed her chair and said, "This is your copy of this book, Carolyn. I bought it for you. Would you just read it and pray about it in regard to the retreat? I was thinking maybe you could help me with it in some way. You have such good ideas about retreats….would you just pray and see what God tells you?"

"Oh, Alice, you are not going to believe what happened when you mentioned that book a little while ago," I told her. "I wrote down the name and intended to buy a copy. I had a feeling I was supposed to do something about it for the retreat–I'll gladly pray and read the book! Maybe I can lead it for you." I blurted out that last part, and embarrassed, I immediately began back-pedaling, trying to set Alice free to select whomever God had chosen as their speaker. Alice was gracious, as always. "We'll both pray," she said, and I promised to help however she wanted. *I will pray, Father, and help me to be sensitive to the role you want me to take for this retreat. Don't let me be presumptuous or assume more than Alice wants. Just let me be your woman, in your place, in your time.*

My next big surprise came when I introduced myself to one of the new faces in leadership: Karen. "Were you in this study last year?" I asked. "I had to drop out after Christmas so I must have missed you."

"I was in Southside last year," she explained.

"Oh, I substitute taught for the teaching director in the Powhatan study last fall. Her son was sick …."

Before I could finish my explanation, she exclaimed excitedly, "Oh! You're the person! I love your lectures. I listened to all of them on CD last fall and you are wonderful! I learned so much …" And she continued singing my accolades.

I was flattered and humbled and we were both surprised to learn of our close connection. In fact, she actually started out in CBS Powhatan last fall in the children's program, but was doing two studies, so she dropped out of the Powhatan one after a week or so. *It is a small world in your family, Heavenly Father, and I'm so grateful to be part of it! Thank you for letting me meet another spiritual sister face to face.*

September 10, Friday

Finally, I Got Eyebrows!

While I was busy sewing my first quilt and knitting a baby sweater set for a friend's new baby, my eyebrows were quietly growing back. They took me quite by surprise about a week ago. I removed makeup at bedtime, cleaned and put away my eyelashes, then stood before the bathroom mirror to brush my teeth. There seemed to be a shadow over my eyes, right where my eyebrows had been drawn on every day for the past couple of months. I leaned in to the mirror for a closer look.

Sure enough, there were itty-bitty eyebrow hairs growing in– lots and lots of them! Enough hairs, in fact, that they cast a dark shadow in my reflection in the regular mirror. I smiled. Then I put on a pair of magnifying eyeglasses to check out my eyelashes. Sure enough, a couple of those peeped through, too, and was I imagining it, or did I see a few more just at the skin's surface edge. I tried not to get too excited because I had eyebrows start in once before in early August, I believe, but they disappeared almost overnight. I tried not to get my hopes up, but really, this was most promising.

Because I was now distracted with quilts and books and knitting as well, I didn't concentrate as much on the missing hair, so I was really pleased in the past couple of days to see a very promising crop of eyebrows growing, accompanied by eyelashes: Double joy! They are still very short, but quite plentiful, so I hope they are here to stay. In fact, some are growing in the spaces I usually tweezed, but I just don't have the heart yet to yank them out. I'm so happy to see eyebrow hair that each and every one is welcome. At some point I'll have to return to tweezing or adapt the Elizabeth Taylor brow, but for right now, they are small and I'm enjoying and cheering on each and every one!

How like you Lord God. Just when I'd about given up hope for eyebrows and lashes, just as I was preparing myself to live with false lashes and heavily penciled pretend brows, you surprise me with a bumper crop of real eyebrows. How often in my life have you restored what I thought was lost once I was willing to stop stewing and look in a new direction? How often have you given me a new direction which was much better than the lost path I had grieved? I can't even count all the times! Thank you, Heavenly Father–Father always does know best!

September 20, Monday

End of the Course

I have known from the first words typed that this book would end–I just wasn't sure how, or when. This month, however, has been a month of change, both in physical ways and in my heart and head as well. I find myself thinking about "back when I had cancer". All during the chemo treatment process, I thought of myself as a woman *with* cancer, although technically, I had been cured on the operating table when all known cancer cells were removed. This month, however, I find myself thinking about when I had cancer–past tense. I am beginning to see my life in time segments: BC–before cancer; AD–after deliverance from cancer; and 2010: the lost year of cancer between BC and AD. But that's okay; it wasn't really a lost year, but a year of living differently, learning new things. It was a year of looking inward and upward in ways I haven't done before. As our church secretary had written in one of her early emails, "In a weird way, with time and with God's hand all over your journey, you will come to say it was one of the best things that happened to you." I'm not at the "best" word yet, but I concede it has been an amazing journey.

I was a cancer patient and now I am not. Of course I'll be followed by various doctors for a long time, and some for the rest of my life. My reconstructive surgeon says I will never be released from her care, and that's okay with me. She's a great artist and I love her creative touch on my body. My general surgeon moved me to a six-month return date and I am excited by that–not that I don't like him, I do! I just feel like I must be doing much better that he doesn't need to see me so often. The surgeon who removed my melanoma declared me a 100% cure last week and told me I don't have to return to his office since someone else will continue to check armpit nodes–so I guess the 100 % cure is being hedged a bit! Still I take all of these changes as signs of health and wellness.

My most dramatic feelings of health and wellness have come in the least important medical ways as the ravages of chemo have left my body: I have eyebrows and eyelashes and oh-so-welcome hair growing back on my head! This month, another wave of scalp hair popped through to the surface and I am thrilled to see no signs of bald spots anywhere, and an identifiable hairline. My hair doesn't even look like it's going to be curly, just my normal fine hair in quantity similar to what I had BC. Of course new individual hairs may still appear, and the ones which are there have a long way to grow before I can go wigless or hatless, but that's okay, I can see the hair at the end of this journey! Hallelujah! I even have hair back on my legs in the normal BC quantities; I just can't remember to shave it! I'll be out in public, look down and see leg hair. I'd love to fancy myself as being mistaken for some progressive European beauty, but I know in those moments I just look like a dowdy old woman. I must get myself back in leg care mode!

And for those of you who wonder: yes, hair is also growing back in that most private place. I just noticed the first little bit of growth a few days ago when the situation there got itchy. When my itchy scalp hair first began to re-appear, it was very distracting especially when wearing a wig. I wanted to snatch that wig off my head and scratch and scratch. But I couldn't do that in public and neither can I scratch the itch in my pubic area. A little hair conditioner cured the head itch, and maybe that's worth a try elsewhere–couldn't hurt anyway and I certainly can't go around scratching that itch! Hair-conditioned pubic hair: Who knew!

Last Wednesday, I entered a new phase of life. I became a mentoring member of the sisterhood of breast cancer. A friend of a friend, newly diagnosed, called me at the urging of our mutual friend. "I see a surgeon tomorrow for the first time– what questions do I ask?" Now I have moved from the woman walking the walk to the woman who has been there, done that, and is willing to hold the hand of a new member in the sisterhood of the pink ribbon. I'm sorry she had to join us, but I'm ever so thankful to be able to speak words of hope and power and encouragement. This phone conversation marked for me an end, and a new beginning. I have hoped to be a blessing to others on this road, and last Wednesday, God gave me that first step on this new highway. And it is sadly, a wide highway with more than 600 women being diagnosed in the United States daily. I don't think God is finished with me in this ministry yet.

On a lighter note, I just returned last night from several days at the beach with Andrew and his girlfriend Christin. It was his fall break from dental school. In early August, when he learned of this early fall break schedule, and wished out loud to go to the beach, I had offered to go with him since his friends would be unavailable–either employed or back in grad school somewhere. Then we learned that Christin's graduate class schedule freed her on Thursdays and Fridays. We went to the condo early Thursday morning. I had a wonderful time. I had been a little bit anxious about this trip, because I remembered the summer vacation as a miserable experience. I hoped that the summer 2010 vacation had not ruined our condo for me for all time.

I need not have worried. The weather was comfortable, I felt great, I could once again entertain myself with indoor activities in the heat of the day and shopping and restaurants and other entertainment in crowds in the evenings–a sharp contrast to the early summer vacation when I was the snappy, irritable chemo patient avoiding any germ potential in my self-imposed cocoon. These past several days, if it weren't for wigs and eyelashes, cancer and chemo would have been just a distant memory. Now I look forward, with great anticipation, to going back next week with Ward. He so deserves a good week there with me as a more pleasant companion and wife than I was in

June! I'm in a new place in life and eager for him to share my new outlook.

Today is Monday. I have spent most of this year keenly aware that we live in a broken world. Over and over I typed the words "we live in a broken world…" or something to that effect. We do, but… I kept running into the "but" word, knowing that God belongs in the rest of that unfinished sentence, but I couldn't find the right words. I could plug his various lessons into that sentence, but as I was in the midst of this adventure, I couldn't get the big picture. I got it as I sat in CBS leadership training ten days ago, listening to some of the many challenges some ladies have faced this past year. I really got it when I realized I am not anxious about my future.

I remember a brief conversation I had with my oncologist at the front end of my chemo journey. "The hard part of this chemo is not knowing if I'll still get cancer back after all this treatment," I said to her, or something along those lines.

She replied, "Well, we don't know that, but what we do know is that you will complete this course of treatment. And if it comes back, we'll treat it again. We have other tools available and we won't give up–we'll keep fighting it."

Those may not be her exact words, but they are close to her comments. I started a journey down the breast cancer road in January. My chemo treatment ended in July. My mind and my heart turned a big corner this month.

We live in a broken world, but God is the God of New Beginnings. Sometimes those beginnings are physical. Some beginnings are called *positive* by the world's standards; some wear a *negative* label by man's reckonings. But with God, all brokenness, whether physical, mental, or emotional, is the opportunity for a new beginning with him. Sometimes new beginnings happen on planet earth, and some initiate in heaven, but all of them have God's hand all over them if we will simply open our eyes along the journey.

In some ways, the year of 2010 has been like a very hard college course that I have lived–and survived! I dealt with each lesson as it was presented. Some chapters were easier, some more challenging, but all were completed in God's time. That course of my life is finished now, tucked up on the shelf of life lessons. I hope my Teacher says, "Well done." I don't know where the next path will lead, but I am confident of the Professor: God of the New Beginnings. My new beginning is currently cancer free; it may not stay that way, but it might.

For the moment, Lord Jesus, I'll enjoy this basket of new beginnings you have placed in my lap. I'll mentor, I'll quilt, I'll serve where you place me. In all possible ways, I'll speak the truth of your Word. Help me to be faithful to complete each task with joy and anticipation of the next phase of my journey. Thank you for all my Mondays. Walk with me now, as I go forth, because... it's Monday.

Chapter 10: INTO A NEW YEAR
The Months After

Getting New Nips

I really thought I had finished my book when I penned the last entry in the September section. Without a doubt, I had moved into a new phase of life. But I was premature in thinking the book was complete. For one thing, I still had one more major reconstructive surgery to get me where I wanted to be in the chest art department. I knew from the beginning that I wanted nipple reconstruction. I had to wait a few months for the new implants to completely heal before that creation could be undertaken. Then I elected to delay surgery until after Christmas. Ward's assistant had to be out until February on maternity leave and I'm his back-up employee. It was fun working with him after so many months of being a "sick" person, but my surgery schedule stretched into early spring.

Finally I was scheduled for the procedure on St. Patrick's Day, March 17. I was tempted to paste big ole shamrock stickers on my breasts where the nipples would be created. I imagined the surprised look on the faces of my doctor and nursing team when they opened my gown. But I had spent two pre-op weeks of washing my chest with antibiotic soap on doctor's orders. Who knows what germs lurk on the glue of "made in China" stickers? I opted not to take the infection risk, but it would have been funny. I had also decided to have a panniculectomy. This is a procedure that removes extra skin, which hangs off the belly like an apron. It is especially common in people who have lost a lot of weight, or had skin stretched out by pregnancies, and I had done both. I decided, with Ward's support, to couple this procedure with the reconstruction. Besides, the extra skin was used as part of the reconstruction graft.

It was a good decision for me and I am well pleased with the results. But it extended my recovery period well past what a simple nipple reconstruction would have done. For one thing, I now had to have drains in my abdomen. My surgeon graciously did liposuction also. My pre-op and post-op instructions informed me to avoid heavy lifting and take it easy on myself. I didn't get the whole picture. I was also not supposed to bend, twist, stretch or put any demands on my lower abdominal area until I was completely healed and the drains were out. Since I didn't realize that, Energizer® Bunny that I am, I did plenty of moving around, just no lifting or heavy pushing on stuff. I even weeded the flower beds in the front of the house. I felt great and the drains kept draining. After about three puzzling weeks, my doctor told me that she wanted me to keep my trunk as immobile as I could and as we talked about that, I realized that I had been doing way too much moving about. After that conversation, I called Ward to pick up anything I dropped or needed from a lower or upper shelf. I felt like a robot with only arms and legs that moved, but I did manage to get rid of the drains the following week. Hallelujah! That was a happy day.

The nipple reconstruction took a surprising turn when the post-op bandages were removed in the office the week after surgery. New nipples are kind of disgusting looking, in my opinion, and I was thankful that I had been shown pictures of what to expect beforehand. For one thing, they pop out of the bandage about the size and shape of a baby boy's penis. Or in case you haven't seen one of those lately, think of a large, fat albino caterpillar. That's what hung off my chest. Only one of them was a deep reddish-purple. Somewhere along the way, the blood supply to this little puppy was impeded. It was not doing well. But the doctor began to work with it and it began to turn pinker. However, it was weeks before I was confident it would ever look close to normal.

Furthermore, I learned that plastic surgery nipples are initially made an outrageous size because they tend to shrink tremendously over the first several months post-op. I'm still in the shrinking stage and have the further assurance that my doctor can revise to a more appropriate size if for some reason they don't get there on their own. I did meet another nurse recently who is also a breast cancer survivor. She works in one of the offices where I get treatment. She encouraged me to be grateful for these current big versions because hers have receded into nothing. I appreciated her candor. I really had not spoken with any previous breast cancer survivors about nipple reconstruction. I was so focused early on with other issues.

I was worried about Ward seeing this latest surgery and for the first several days after surgery and bandage removal, I managed to arrange my bathing and clothes changing times when he wasn't around. Finally I said, "Do you want to see my new nipples? They're pretty disgusting looking. I think I look like a porn star."

"Have you ever seen a porn star?" he asked. I think he was a little worried.

"No," I laughed. "But I think they probably look outrageous, and these nipples definitely look outrageous right now!" Bless his heart, he managed to not look repulsed and even had some encouraging words for me. What a sweet man!

Several breast cancer survivors whom I had met early in my treatment either had lumpectomies or elected not to get nipple reconstruction. Some women opt instead for tattoos to simulate nipples and areolas. Some choose nothing. Both of these options make bra shopping easy. I have gone through a small fortune trying to find bras and padding and bandages, which permit the nipples to remain erect through the healing process. Furthermore, I have sensitive skin and I've had a few reactions to some products. One of my friends, a nursing mother, seemed genuinely pleased when I passed along a nearly full box of maternity nursing pads I no longer needed. These two little nipples have managed to consume a whole lot of attention, but I'm still glad I chose this route. When I look in the mirror I look pretty good to me, relatively speaking. I see a whole person, not a cancer victim. I feel finished, as in "end construction zone."

I feel exceedingly blessed. A few years ago, women didn't have many options, and breast reconstruction was nonexistent. *Thank you, God, for doctors who work tirelessly to help us move forward.* When I first met my plastic surgeon, she gave me a packet of information about reconstruction options. It began with these words: "I cannot give you back what you have lost…" Well, Doctor, thank you for giving me a beautiful facsimile.

Exercise–Who Knew!

On November 7th of my treatment year, the day before my birthday, Ward and I joined a local gym. It wasn't a birthday present. In fact, I was practically dragged there kicking and screaming. Ward was aware of the statistics, which suggest that exercise reduces the likelihood of breast cancer recurrence. He had asked me several times when I was going to start exercising, and I always managed to find an excuse. Finally, he brought the topic up again and made it clear he was rather aggravated with my excuses. I learned the term "aggravated" the first year we were married. We got into a little tiff, and I later said something about Ward having been mad at me. "I was not mad," he insisted. "I was simply aggravated; I don't get mad."

Fast forward 25 years and Ward was aggravated with me about exercise. I don't like it when anyone is "aggravated" with me, so we joined the gym. Mostly, I think I joined because if the cancer comes back, I don't want to wear the guilt of thinking, "If only I'd exercised, I might not have cancer." I also never wanted to hear my sweet husband say, "If only you had exercised…."

The first weeks were really hard, but I was determined to get in the five hours per week that the doctors prescribed. I used weight machines and I worked on the treadmill. Occasionally I rode a stationary bike. The treadmills and bikes were equipped with TVs so I entertained myself with that mind-numbing media. Actually, if I could find a good football game or later in the year basketball, I had fun watching them. In fact, my alma mater accommodated me by making it to the final four in basketball, so I had lots of opportunities to get into the game while racking up exercise hours for myself. Sometimes I watched a home decorating show instead. Those can be a little slow, so I learned to also read a book during commercials and boring segments.

Throughout the winter I kept up my exercise pace, usually doing at least six hours per week. Somewhere along the way, I discovered I really liked exercising–oh, not the work of it, nor the sweat, nor the time commitment. But I was pleased with my progress. Something in me now wouldn't let me stop; ego, or stubbornness, or I don't know what. I just know I made exercise a priority and I kept doing it. My oncologist was shocked and pleased when she asked me about exercise during one of my check-ups and learned how diligently I worked. "I wish more of my patients would follow this advice," she said.

Sometime in February, I finally felt I had enough hair to lay aside the baseball cap I had worn for work outs. I also took my first water aerobics class. It was fun. I tried a couple of other classes, too. They were fun. I made friends there. For the first time in my life, I felt that I actually belonged in that space. I still exercise regularly. I've reached a point now that if I don't exercise, I miss it. It makes me feel better mentally. I also see that I am stronger and I'm getting more flexible. I never expected to hear these words come out of my mouth, much less mean them. But there it is. I've become a bit of a gym rat. Who knew!

Pains and Anxiety

As I strove to challenge myself more physically, I ventured onto the elliptical machines. I upped the speed on the treadmill and raised the angle of the walk. I began walking through my hilly neighborhood pushing myself faster and harder. I also started swimming laps. I thought if I was going to invest the time to exercise, I'd like it to be as challenging, and therefore calorie burning, as possible. Then I began to experience pain in my back. Two things about the pain bothered me: one, it wasn't the usual lower back pain that I had experienced off and on for years. And two, I did all the things I knew to treat the symptoms, but the pain didn't get better. In fact, it got worse.

I called my oncologist and they got me into her office immediately. A series of x-rays and blood tests were done stat and within twenty-four hours, I had my answer. I had degenerative disc disease. I was ecstatic! I was elated! I was relieved. Like many cancer survivors, the least little abnormality raises the fear that cancer has sprung up in some other part of the body. I was so happy to have degenerative discs. I could live with that diagnosis and that was the major gift: I could live.

I led the winter women's retreat for my Bible study's leadership the following weekend delighted to be serving God and the women who are such important people in my life. I told the story of my eventful week. In fact, Alice, the Associate Teaching Director, had worked closely with me to get this retreat together. She had called me earlier in the week as I was in the midst of my little scare. "Don't be afraid, Carolyn," she answered when I told her of my pending medical appointment. "This is going to turn out fine. I think the enemy is just trying to frighten you. Don't be afraid."

"But I am afraid, Alice," I replied.

"I know," she said. And she prayed with me on the phone. I continued preparations for the retreat. It would not have mattered what the diagnosis was, I was going to do the retreat.

That's the place I am now in this stage of my life. There will be times when I am afraid. There will be times when I feel threatened by the fear of cancer or some other life challenged. But I intend not to let such thoughts dominate my life. Instead, I look forward to my tomorrows, confident that God's grace is sufficient for this day and for those days which follow this one.

Slow Growing Hair

Each individual's experience with cancer is unique in some ways. Each woman deals with the disease in her own way with the particular personality, mindset, and spiritual perspective with which she is blessed. In the big scheme of things, medical personnel can give a general pattern for how treatment and recovery can be expected to progress. But it's just a general, generic estimate. My hair growth was a good example. It took months and months to reach the very short point where I was willing to leave off the wig for anything besides exercise.

In January, I went to work in Ward's office each day wearing my favorite wig. Then one day I got my courage up to leave the wig at home and transition to my very short hairstyle. One of his patients, the adult daughter of a fellow church member, came in that day for the second appointment of her multi-appointment treatment plan. She complimented me on my new haircut unaware that I had been on chemo and was just getting my own hair back on my head. I smiled and thanked her without explanation. But I felt like a freshly shorn sheep. I wasn't comfortable with such short hair, so I put the wig back on to await more hair growth. Some days passed and one morning as I looked at the schedule, I was surprised to see this same patient back for her third treatment. I wondered what she would say when I had longer hair again, so I made a little plan with my husband. Sure enough, as I seated her, she commented on my hair. I said, "Oh, were you in here last week when my twin sister was working? She has really short hair." For a few moments, I had great fun with her confusion, but I couldn't keep it up for long. I started laughing and told her my story. She was a good sport and the rest of the appointment was pleasantly uneventful.

My hair grew back so slowly that I didn't have my first real haircut until June of 2011, nearly a year after chemo ended. I'd had a couple of simple trims around the edges at my neckline and ears, but my bangs and the top of my head took their own sweet time to grow out. Surprisingly, my hair also came back with the same texture and tendency to curl as pre-chemo. For me, that meant it would curl when short and wet, but dried straight and flat. I have learned to put mousse in when it's wet, let it air dry and polish it off with styling wax and hair spray. That way I keep curls or waves all day with little effort. But if I had hoped to grow shoulder length hair like I used to wear, I think it would take some years. I think I may hold the record for slow growing hair, about a quarter inch a month it seems.

The color also surprised me, but not greatly. I've colored my hair for years, since the boys were small, so I really didn't know what color it would be. I was well prepared to continue with the coloring routine I had always used, but I used a permanent color product. Then I learned from my oncologist that post-chemo hair is initially too fragile for such products. My hair grew in dark, dark gray. It was shocking and made me look haggard. I scurried to find a semi-permanent color and started coloring my hair long before I abandoned the wig. I couldn't stand looking in the mirror at the old lady who looked back. Today I wear my hair several shades darker than the blond shades I had favored pre-chemo and am generally pleased with my new look. As my friend Lynn said, "There are no bad hair days after chemo." I couldn't agree with her more.

Lessons and Blessings

In one sense, there are no bad days after chemo. Each day is a blessing and an opportunity to interact with those I love, greet old friends and make new ones, try new things, or enjoy doing something that is familiar and fun. Sure, there are days when sad things happen, events I'd rather not have to face, like the death of a loved one, or other life disappointments, but the fact is, they are still days that I'm living and enjoying just being alive.

When I look back over the journey from diagnosis through treatment and recovery, I see that it was a year of lessons and blessings and amazing experiences along the way. I learned that although we live in a broken world, God is still in control of the big picture and the little details. Over and over God reminded me that he holds my times in his hands. Repeatedly, God poured his blessings upon me. He sent all kinds of people to minister to me: Friends and strangers, professionals and lay people, fellow pilgrims on the pink ribbon journey and people just passing briefly through my life. Along the way, he also gave me the privilege to be a blessing to others, and I pray that such opportunities continue to materialize. I believe that they will, because God rarely calls us to live in isolation.

God's blessings were also often tangible: cards, gifts, food, flowers and time people spent with me and for me to make my burden light. Great medical care was also a tangible blessing.

I developed some new skills: I can now put on false eyelashes within a couple of minutes and I know how to draw great looking eyebrows using an assorted color collection of pencils (power over the finished product to set it). God gave me lots of opportunities to enjoy humor along the way and he sent me sweet distractions, like obsessing over missing hair instead of missing boobs!

God also taught me to exercise an increased measure of mercy and grace toward others, recognizing that most of us are doing our best to get through this broken world. He challenged me to be open and vulnerable so that I may be a blessing to others and he reminded me that it is not my job to judge.

Every Day is Monday

Finally, God has taught me that every day is Monday. As I moved through the cancer experience, I began to realize that Monday represents new beginnings and fresh starts. The Bible says God's mercies are new every morning.[1] God continually gives us new beginnings because of his mercy and grace poured onto and into our lives. He calls us to daily renewal and refreshment in his spirit.

In that sense, this book never ends, because with God, it's always Monday.

---

1   *Lamentations 3:22-24*

About the Author:

Carolyn Mustian

Carolyn was just looking for an interesting job or volunteer position for the empty-nest years as her two sons neared college graduation. What she got instead was a disease that strikes one in eight women: breast cancer. Her experiences coping with cancer blossomed from a journal into a book of hope, encouragement and new beginnings. Along the way, she discovered there are amazing lessons, blessings, and opportunities for spiritual and emotional growth on the pink ribbon road. She also learned new skills to cope with the effects of chemotherapy, like how to draw eyebrows (use two or three different colors of brow pencil and set it with powder), how to apply false eyelashes, where to find a great wig (and some not so great ones), and how to use a double mastectomy as an opportunity to get the chest size you always wanted! Who says you can't find some fun and funny on the pink ribbon road?

Carolyn also found that the treatment phase of breast cancer can be an invitation to look at life from a different perspective at an altered pace. It was a chance to grow in ways she had not dreamed. Today, Carolyn is a quilter, an author, a speaker, and office manager of a large medical practice where she has an opportunity to interact with women on a daily basis, some of whom also face a breast cancer diagnosis. She and her husband, Ward, live in Richmond with their cat, Bubbles. Ward is a dentist in private practice and their sons, Andrew and David, now college grads, live nearby. Carolyn sees each new day as an opportunity to celebrate life.

For more information or to contact Carolyn to speak at your women's event, please follow her blog at MondaysJourney.com or contact her directly at CarolynMustian@msn.com.